Canary Islands

Berlitz Publishing Company, Inc.

Princeton   Mexico City   Dublin   Eschborn   Singapore

Text:	Norman Renouf
Editor:	Media Content Marketing, Inc.
Photography:	Chris Coe
Cover Photo:	Chris Coe
Photo Editor:	Naomi Zinn
Layout:	Media Content Marketing, Inc.
Cartography:	Ortelius Design

ISBN 2-8315-7690-3

Printed in Italy
010/009 REV

CONTENTS

● A (☛) in the text denotes a highly recommended sight

Canary Islands

THE ISLANDS AND
THE PEOPLE

More than 1,000 km (620 miles) south of the Iberian Peninsula, just 115 km (71 miles) from the nearest point on the African coast, an archipelago of thirteen volcanic islands jut dramatically from the Atlantic Ocean. These, the Canary Islands — politically an integral part of Spain — together with a small area of the western part of Africa, the Azores, Madeira, the Savage islands and Cape Verde, form the region known as Macronesia. Six of the islands, Alegranza, La Graciosa, Lobos, Montaña Clara, Roque del Este and Roque del Oeste, are no less than specks in the sea and remain uninhabited. Of the others, the three closest to Africa; Gran Canaria, Lanzarote and Fuerteventura, are geologically the oldest and as they have the most extensive coastal shelf, they also boast the largest number of beaches. The four western islands, Tenerife, La Palma, La Gomera and El Hierro, in descending order of size, have coastlines that often have cliffs rising vertiginously out of the ocean. However, only Tenerife has beaches of any size and the golden sands have usually been imported from the Sahara or rescued from the bottom of the sea. In total, the archipelago has approximately 1,500 km (930 miles) of seacoast, and the characteristic intensely blue waters are due to the ocean's depth — as much as 3,000 m (9,840 ft) between some of the islands.

Geographically within the bounds of the Tropic of Cancer, the surrounding ocean is somewhat cooler than would be expected at such a sub-tropical latitude. The Gulf Current arrives from the north and the ensuing trade winds that brush the islands brings to the Canaries, at sea level at least, a most genial climate indeed. Average temperatures on the beach vary around 19° Celsius (66°F) in winter and 25° Celsius (77°F) in summer. However, as many of the islands are mountainous — Mount Teide on Tenerife rises to 3,718 m (12,195 ft) and not only dominates the archipelago but is the highest mountain in Spain — the temperatures can vary dramatically not only between islands, but on islands as well.

The combination of such a climate and the unusual geological features have given rise to an amazing array of flora and fauna, which thrives even though not one of the islands has a running river. The isolation of the archipelago has also played its part in the preservation of these natural gifts. In fact, with around 650 native species, it is one of the most important areas in the world, comparable only with several other archipelagos, such as Hawaii and the Galapagos. Recognizing this, and intent upon preserving it, the Law of Natural Areas in the Canaries has created nature and rural parks, nature reserves, nature monuments, protected landscapes, and areas of scientific interest with the intent of limiting human activity in the zones. These amount to no less than 36% of the archipelago's territory.

But what about the people of the Canary Islands? Governed by the Spanish since the end of the 15th century the Canarians, to outsiders, look Spanish, speak Spanish, are imbued with Spanish culture and to all intents and purposes are little different — perhaps with exception of being a somewhat quieter of character, than their mainland cousins. However, throughout the centuries the Canary Islands have acted as a bridge between Europe, Africa, and the Americas, and as a consequence have become home to any number of people originating from disparate cultures. And the result, today, is a people that think of themselves as very much Canarian first and Spanish second.

Capturing El Rey — only the brave will join the local chess players in the Parque de Santa Catalina.

They have learned also, in the second half of the 20th century, to capitalize on the islands' natural resources, in this case the fine climate and beaches that attract so many visitors from northern Europe and other, less likely destinations. It comes as a surprise, especially given the former Soviet Union's well-known dire economic problems, that many of the brochures advertising tourist attractions now include descriptions in Russian. Tourism is, indeed, a massive business. The Department of Tourism and Transport reported that in the first ten months of 1999, over eight million foreign tourists entered the Canaries, an increase of more than 600,000 during that period of the previous year! Close to three million headed for Tenerife, two and a half to Gran Canaria, one and a half to Lanzarote and just over one million to Fuerteventura. La Palma attracted a paltry 106,880.

While certain areas, notably the southern coasts of Gran Canaria and Tenerife, and to a lesser but growing extent Lanzarote and Fuerteventura, cater to mass tourism, the smaller islands that lack commercially exploitable beaches will always lag well behind in numbers, if not in their natural attractions. It would seem that with such numbers, the islands would be perpetually crowded, but this is not so as most visitors head directly for the major resorts, such as Playa de las Américas on Tenerife and Playa del Inglés on Gran Canaria. In fact, if all the land devoted to tourism were to be added up, it would still occupy only a mere fraction of the islands' total area and natural wealth.

So which is the best island for you? It may be a cliché — but it is nonetheless true, that there is an island for all tastes. The diversity of landscapes on the islands is quite amazing.

Snow capped mountains, beautiful verdant valleys, deserts, towering cliffs and wonderful beaches of yellow or black sand; all can be found in the Canaries, and some islands have intriguing combinations of these characteristics. Remember, the Canaries are volcanic islands, and volcanic islands are never dull. La Palma erupted as recently as 1971. On Lanzarote you can not

Bursts of vibrant color can be found throughout the barren volcanic landscape.

only gaze at the awesome scenery created by earth-shattering events that occurred centuries ago, you can also watch your lunch cooking now over the heat of the volcano beneath your feet (see page 141)

Tenerife is the biggest island, and has plenty to show for it. In Mount Teide it features the grandest scenery and it certainly has the greatest number of tourist attractions by day and night. In terms of all-round appeal, however, Gran Canaria runs a close second. Both have bustling new cities and sleepy old towns to visit; both have wonderful and strikingly beautiful interiors; and both have modern resorts ranging from good-time to quiet-time. If a long stretch of golden beach is a priority, then Gran Canaria has the edge. Lanzarote, with its stark *malpaís* (badlands), will delight those people who are environmentally aware yet enjoy the company of other tourists; however, whether or not the continued growth of tourism there erodes this delicate balance remains to be seen. But the tourist attractions masterminded by design guru César Manrique combine well with those of resorts like Puerto del Carmen, and the general ambience of this island with its low-rise, whitewashed buildings is very appealing. Fuerteventura tends to polarize opinion: it is truly a desert island — wind-swept, sandy, and barren. Is it an oasis in the middle of an over-complicated world, as some have claimed, or is it simply the desert of its first impression? The beaches here are certainly the best in the Canaries, and resorts to suit most tastes are springing up. Watersports aside, there isn't much else to do or see. The lesser known and much smaller islands of La Palma, La Gomera and El Hierro do not, surprisingly, have that many beaches and have therefore escaped mass tourism and will continue to do so. The lack of attractions that this brings in its wake has, in these three charming islands, become an attraction in itself.

There are relatively few hotels and restaurants of note (although enough for discerning visitors), no discos and blaring bars to disturb the night's peace, and best of all — as far as many are concerned — almost no tourists. They do have a bountiful supply of beautiful mountainous scenery, and if you search hard enough, a pleasant beach or two to relax on. And if this is your idea of a perfect vacation, then one of these islands may be your Shangri-La. For most people, though, a day or two away from it all is enough. Island hopping is relatively easy and a few days on an unspoiled island combined with the creature comforts of a major resort offer the best of both worlds. Travel independently, look around the corner from the next hotel, and you will soon discover that there is much more to the Canary Islands than just another winter suntan.

Santa Cruz de Tenerife, capital of the Canary Islands, is modern yet still retains a quaint island charm.

A BRIEF HISTORY

The Canary Islands are a land of legends. The ancient Greeks thought of them as the Garden of Hesperides, Romans called this archipelago the Fortunate Islands, and Homer tells us that blessed ones were sent to the Elysian Fields to enjoy eternal happiness in a land where winter was unknown. Could this have been the Canaries?

The author Plutarch wrote of fertile lands somewhere off the coast of Africa, where the breezes of springtime never stop. His source was the Roman leader Sertorius, who had heard of the lands from an explorer.

Many writers link the lost continent of Atlantis with the Canaries. According to Plato this rich, happy land, lying somewhere to the west of Gibraltar in the Atlantic Ocean, was destroyed by earthquakes and tidal waves nearly 12,000 years ago. After the cataclysm only the mountaintops of Atlantis remained above the sea and constituted seven islands. The Canaries perhaps?

From Plato to Jules Verne the possibilities have stirred people's imagination, ranging from the theories of learned academics to the ramblings of wild eccentrics. By now the truth is surely lost in the myths and mists of time. What is undeniable, however, is the magical presence that these seven volcanic sisters possess. When you sight Mount Teide on a distant horizon you will understand the profusion of legends.

The First Inhabitants

Long before the first European sailors beached in the Canaries, all seven islands were inhabited. The original Canarians came to be called Guanches, meaning in the native tongue "man." Strictly speaking, this name applies only to the original inhabitants of Tenerife.

The Castillo de San José on Lanzarote bears witness to the repeated conquests of the Canary Islands.

The Guanches are thought to have arrived in the islands around the 1st or 2nd century B.C., probably from North Africa. Ethnographers link them with the Cro-Magnon and Proto-Mediterranean race. They were tall, light-skinned, often blue-eyed and blond-haired. You can see their remains in the meticulous collection of the Museo Canario in Las Palmas on Gran Canaria. Here too you can study their pre-occupation with death. Like the ancient Egyptians they carefully embalmed their dead, presumably for a ceremonial passage to the next world. Cryptic rock carvings have been found that may explain these rituals, but so far no one has found the Canarian version of the Rosetta Stone with which to decipher them.

Another baffling mystery is how the Guanches arrived on the islands. No evidence of Guanche boats has ever been discovered; so were they marooned here by pirates or perhaps exiled by their own people? One theory is that they may have floated across from North Africa on reed craft. The expeditions of Thor Heyerdahl do lend some credence to this idea, and the concept is explored in great detail at the Pyramids of Güímar on Tenerife.

In keeping with their Berber origins the Guanches were cave dwellers, though by no means did all Guanches live in the rocks, and many of the original caves that remain today (for example the Cuevas de Valerón on Gran Canaria) were probably used only for storage. Cave dwelling in such a climate is a logical idea, being cooler in summer and warmer in winter than more conventional accommodations. Even today, there are many cave dwellings in the islands.

A Guanche legacy that you will see at the market place and in traditional eating houses is *gofio*, a finely-ground, toasted flour that is still a traditional Canarian staple. The Guanche language also lives on in such place names as Tafira and Tamadaba (on Gran Canaria), Timanfaya (on Lanzarote), Teide (on Tenerife), and Tenerife itself.

Conquistadors

The first foreign visitors to the Canaries are thought to have been Arab sailors who landed on Gran Canaria some 2,000 years ago and were met warmly. In later centuries the islanders' gracious hospitality was to cost them dearly.

Europeans did not arrive until the 14th century, when the Genoese sailor Lanzarotto Marcello colonized the island, known then in native tongue as Tytheroygatra and subsequently as Lanzarote. Slave traders, treasure seekers, and missionaries all followed in Lanzarotto's wake, but it was not until 1402 that the European conquest of the Canaries began in earnest. At its helm was the Norman baron, Jean de Béthencourt, under service to Henry III, king of Castile. After the baron had taken Lanzarote and Fuerteventura with comparative ease, his ships were scattered by storms off Gran Canaria. He next turned to El Hierro, where the awestruck islanders welcomed the new visitors arriving in their great floating vessels as gods. Béthencourt returned the hospitality by inviting the natives aboard his ships. He then took them captive and sold them into slavery.

Around this time the Portuguese, who had also been colonizing the Atlantic, turned their attention to the Canaries. Naval skirmishes ensued between the two powers, but at the end of the war of succession between Portugal and Castile, the wide-ranging Treaty of Alcaçovas ended Lisbon's claims to the Fortunate Islands.

By order of Ferdinand and Isabella of Castile, the second phase of the conquest was set in motion. By 1483 Gran Canaria had been subdued and in 1488 Gomera was taken. La Palma held out until 1493, and after another two years of furious fighting, the biggest prize of all, Tenerife, was in Spanish hands. The process of pacification and conversion to the Christian faith had taken almost a century of bloody guerilla warfare with thousands of casualties, sustained mainly on the brave but ill-equipped Guanche side.

The World Is Round!

Just as the conquest of the Canaries was reaching its climax, Christopher Columbus (Cristobal Colón in Spanish) was planning his historic expedition in search of a sea route to the East Indies. Each of the Canaries boasts some connection with Columbus, who came to the islands because they were then the world's most westerly charted points and therefore the last stopping point before venturing into the unknown.

The great navigator definitely stopped off at Gomera and Las Palmas on his voyage of 1492, and he even recorded a volcanic eruption while passing Tenerife. Not surprisingly his crew took this as an ill omen, but as history tells us, once past El Hierro they did not drop off the edge of the world after all. Columbus's routes and Canarian connections may be traced at the atmospheric Casa de Colón in Las Palmas (see page 55).

The role of the islands as a bridge between the Old World and the New World

A bust of Columbus looks out over Vegueta — his jumping off point for the Americas.

has continued through the centuries. Canarians have settled in Latin America in large numbers, usually in search of a better way of life, and news from Venezuela and Cuba is treated almost as a local item in the Canary Islands newspapers. Canarian bananas provided the stock for those of the Carribbean, and in spoken accent and musical rhythms the Canaries lie halfway between Spain and South America.

Wine and Warfare

The Canaries' first major agricultural enterprise was sugar. Sugar cane sprouted easily on the islands, and during the first half of the 16th century a burgeoning industry developed. Boom turned to bust, however, with cheaper sugar production from Brazil and the Antilles, and the industry died.

Still, trade links had at least been established with both the Old and the New World, and wine became the new farming venture to bolster the economy. Grapes grown in the volcanic soil produced a distinctive, full-bodied malmsey wine *(malvasía)* that became the fashionable drink of aristocratic Europe. Shakespeare and Voltaire, among others, were lavish in their praise, and today's island visitors can still sample the excellent wine in *bodegas*, restaurants, or even from the *supermercado*. When touring the islands you may still see old disused wine presses *(lagares)* on hillsides.

By the end of the 18th century the Canaries were a sufficiently important trading point to attract all types of

Agriculture is still an important part of the economy here, as the climate is ideal for many exotic crops.

pirates. In 1797, Horatio Nelson attacked Santa Cruz de Tenerife in search of a Spanish treasure ship. The defenders responded vigorously, accounting for the lives of 226 British sailors and the removal of the lower part of Nelson's saluting arm. The Santa Cruzeros clearly had no hard feelings towards Admiral Nelson, however. Once it was known that the attack had been repelled, a gift of wine was sent out to Nelson (England was, after all, an important wine market) and a street was named Calle de Horacio Nelson in his honor!

Free Trade

By the early 18th century Canarians had become fully Spanish in both outlook and loyalties, and many volunteers joined the Peninsular War (Spaniards call it the War of Independence) which ended in 1814 with the restoration of Ferdinand VII to the Spanish throne.

Economic problems arose in the early 19th century, and the wine industry started to fail. Luckily another single-crop opportunity presented itself in the form of cochineal, a parasitic insect attracted to the *opuntia* variety of cactus. The tiny bodies of the female bugs contain a dark-red liquid perfect for dyeing, and for 50 years or so, millions of bugs were crushed for the sake of the Canarian economic good.

The Bug Bubble burst with the rise of chemical dyes in the 1870s. With the failure of yet another mono-culture, the Spanish government felt constrained to help the Canarian economy. In the mid-19th century, free port status was granted by royal decree to one port in each of the islands (two in Tenerife). The lowering of duties and trade barriers at a time of considerable shipping expansion had the desired effect, and Santa Cruz de Tenerife and Las Palmas soon became two of the world's busiest ports.

The most recent major crop to come from the Canaries is bananas. The variety is the dwarf banana, small and very tasty, and today demand actually outstrips production in some areas. The first exports were made in the 1880s and the banana has continued to be a mainstay of the islands' economy. Despite some recent problems and concern for the future, it is hoped that bananas will continue to be an important Canarian crop alongside their other staples; tomatoes and potatoes.

In 1912, *Cabildos* (Island Councils) were created and given the responsibility for the social, political and economic administration of each island, and co-ordination with the Town Halls. This led, in 1927, to the islands being divided into two provinces; Santa Cruz de Tenerife with the islands of Tenerife, La Palma, La Gomera and El Hierro; and Las Palmas de Gran Canaria with the islands of Lanzarote and Fuerteventura.

The Spanish Civil War

The plot that sparked off the Spanish Civil War was hatched in the Canary Islands. In 1936 a group of senior officers, discontented with the policies of the Spanish Republican Government, met in secret in the woods of La Esperanza on Tenerife. They had come to meet a fellow officer, Francisco Franco, whom the government had banished to the Canaries for subversive plotting. From the Canaries, Franco took off for North Africa, the launching pad for the insurgent right-wing attack.

Three years later his armies had triumphed in a ruthless struggle that cost hundreds of thousands of Spanish lives. The Canaries were not spared the horrors of the war (mass Republican executions took place in the aptly named *Barranco del Infierno,* the Gorge of Hell, on Tenerife), but on the whole the islands prospered during Franco's period of dictatorship, which provided for added protection to their free-port status.

Tourism

The massive growth of tourism in the islands since the 1960s has, in some cases, literally refaced the landscape, with brand-new resorts such as Playa de las Américas on Tenerife and Playa del Inglés on Gran Canaria, springing up like Gold Rush boom towns. However, such developments are mostly the exception and whole swathes of even the more developed islands are virtually untouched, while La Palma, La Gomera and El Hierro are only now starting to provide even the most basic tourist facilities. The infrastruc-

This view of the Castle at Garachico showcases Tenerife's natural beauty.

ture and transport systems both within and between the islands have, as a consequence, improved drastically.

In 1972 the passing of the *Régimen Económico y Fiscal* (Economic and Tax Regime) allowed for different methods of tax collection and economic management than that of the rest of Spain. Three years later, after the death of Franco, a constitutional monarchy was restored with King Juan Carlos I at its head. However, the subsequent de-colonization of Spain's Western Sahara possession resulted in a movement of many thousands of people back to the Canary Islands, creating social and logistical problems. The year 1978 saw the declaration of a new Spanish Constitution, further strength-

This memorial at Santa Cruz de Tenerife offers a beautiful view of the outlying islands.

ening the new democracy and preparing the ground for a State of Autonomous Regions. As a result, on 16 August 1982 the Canary Islands were given autonomous status, with nearly all governmental functions transferred from Madrid and the status of capital being shared between Santa Cruz de Tenerife and Las Palmas de Gran Canaria. The former is the head office of the Canarian Parliament, where the President of the Canary Islands is elected and half the departments and ministries are based; and the latter is the seat of the presidency of the government and the home of the superior courts and the remaining departments and ministries. The Canary Islands Parliament has 60 members distributed equally between the two provinces; with Tenerife, La Palma, La Gomera and El Hierro having 15, 8, 4 and 3 respectively, and Gran Canaria, Lanzarote and Fuerteventura having 15, 8 and 7 respectively. Each island still has its own *Cabildo* (Island Council), and all officials are elected by a free vote every four years. The full incorporation of Spain into the European Economic Community in 1990 brought the end of the duty-free ports status, but saw certain special allowances for the Canary Islands with respect to agriculture, fishing and taxes.

WHERE TO GO

PROVINCE OF SANTA CRUZ DE TENERIFE:
Tenerife, El Hierro, La Gomera and La Palma (telephone code 928):

TENERIFE
Area: 2,046 sq km (790 sq miles) — the largest island.
Population: 666,000

Tenerife is not only the largest of the Canaries geographically, it also offers the tourist more sights, more attractions, more towns and cities to explore, and more contrasts than any of the other islands. Where else can you look around a banana plantation and then take a short drive half-way up a mountain for a snowball fight?

Tenerife has been welcoming visitors from cold northern climes since the 19th century. However, the focus has changed from the cloudy, green north coast where Puerto de la Cruz was once the favorite resort (it is still enormously popular), to the hot, dry, arid south.

Santa Cruz de Tenerife

The capital of Tenerife and the administrative center for the westerly Canaries, Santa Cruz is not a city in which tourists spend a great deal of time. The main square is the **Plaza de España,** in the middle of which stands a four-sided cross, a memorial to the dead of the Spanish Civil War. The huge, drab, gray building adjacent to the Plaza is the Cabildo Insular (local government headquarters) which also houses the tourist office and the **Museo Arqueológico,** with important exhibits illustrating the life and death rituals of Guanche society (see page 13). The museum is open Tuesday–Sunday 10am–8pm and the entrance fee is a mere 400 pesetas (free on Sundays). Back on the seafront, discover the **Iglesia Matriz de la Concepción** (Church of the Immaculate Conception). Dating from the early 16th century, this is the town's most important historical building and contains several interesting relics, including Nelson's faded battle flag.

Puerto de la Cruz

Puerto, as this town is often abbreviated to, has neither good beaches nor the abundant sunshine of the south, yet for many travelers it is the most complete resort on the island. It has been attracting convalescing northern Europeans for over a century and it maintains much of its colonial grandeur. The seafront promenade has been quite heavily commercialized but not at all spoiled, and the atmosphere is always lively

Frisky dolphins are one of many reasons to visit Loro Parque in Puerto de la Cruz.

without being boisterous. The main square, **Plaza de Charco**, is the hub of both tourist and local life, and its numerous cafés, restaurants, and shops are busy at all hours. Just off the square, the old town around the Puerto Pesquero is remarkably oblivious to change. Among the narrow streets with faded wooden balconies and carved doors are the **Casa de Miranda**, now a crafts shop and restaurant, and, oldest of all, the **Casa de la Real Aduana** (Customs House), built in 1620, facing the tiny port.

The problem of Puerto's lack of a decent beach was brilliantly addressed by the late César Manrique who designed **Lago Martiánez,** which is open daily 9:45am to 5pm. This 3-hectare (8-acre) complex of tropical lagoons, cascading fountains and sunbathing terraces is cleverly landscaped with lush palms and black-and-white volcanic rocks to fit perfectly into the seafront, where the surf crashes spectacularly against the rocks.

There are numerous places on Tenerife competing for the attention of tourists, but there is one, just to the west of Puerto, that absolutely should not be missed. **Loro Parque;** (open daily 8:30am–5pm, admission: 2,900 ptas, €17.43) has the world's largest collection of parrots — more than 300 species and subspecies. It is also home to the most eclectic array of animals including gorillas, chimpanzees, tigers, jaguars, alligators, sea-lions, dolphins and numerous other creatures that are exhibited in carefully and creatively, designed spaces. Look also for the underwater world of the aquarium and shark tunnel, and the newest, and undoubtedly most inventive display. The Planet Penguin, the largest Penguinarium in the world, covers 3,900 square m (nearly 1 acre) and has been created as a natural habitat for these engaging creatures. The temperature of their iceberg is kept at between -2° and 2° C (28°–36° F) with 12 tons of artificial snow falling on it daily through openings in the roof. The surrounding sea is chilled to 10° C (50° F). Visitors are conveyed around on a moving walkway that allows the King, Gentoo and Rockhopper penguins to be seen cavorting on land and in the water. Look also for the dolphin, sea lion, and parrot shows, and animal feedings.

Just north of Puerto, on the road to La Orotavo, there are two places, both open daily 9am–6pm, that have similar themes, but exhibit them in rather different ways. The oldest of these, and closest to town, is undoubtedly the **Jardín Botánico** (Botanical Garden), founded by royal decree in 1788. Covering some 2.5 hectares (6 acres), it has palms of every variety and the centerpiece is a huge South American fig tree whose enormous branches and roots have become intertwined into one great tree house. Further on, **Bananera El Guanche** provides fascinating insight into how a Canarian banana plantation operates. By way of a multi-lingual introductory video show, a surprisingly informative and entertaining brochure, and exhibits in its 12,000-sq-m (nearly 3-acre) park which boasts, besides nu-

Canaries

You don't have to be an expert, or a canary, to tell the difference between a male and a female canary. Only the male knows how to sing.

Canaries, the most famous wildlife found in the islands, take their name from the archipelago, and not vice versa. They are also found on Madeira and the Azores.

Serinus canaria was first imported to Europe in the 16th century. Originally they were colorless birds, but breeders in Europe were able to develop a yellow variety and other festive colors followed. Your chances of spotting wild canaries today are slim. Look instead in the cages attached to the outside of houses in smaller towns and villages.

merous bananas, a superb collection of exotic trees, shrubs, flowers, and cacti from all over the world (open daily 9am–6pm; admission 1,000 ptas, €6.01).

La Orotava is a remarkably well-preserved, unspoiled old town set on a steep hill high above its old port, Puerto de la Cruz. Stately mansions, ancient churches, and cobbled streets are its trademarks. The twin towers, Baroque façade, and Byzantine dome of the **Iglesia Nuestra Señora de la Concepción** dominate a fascinating skyline that has remained virtually unchanged for centuries. Continue on up Calle San Francisco to the **Casas**

An aloe flower blooms at the botanical garden, located in Puerto de la Cruz.

de los Balcones (Houses of the Balconies). The balconies in question are inside the house's courtyard and are some of the finest examples of their kind. This splendid 17th-century mansion and the Casa de Turista (built in 1590) opposite are now shops dedicated to Canary handicrafts.

North of Puerto

El Sauzal is important for its wines, and this industry is shown to its best effect at the **Casa del Vino "La Baranda"** (open Tuesday–Saturday 11am–8pm and Sundays and holidays 11am–6pm, admission free). See how the wine is made

On the descent into Garachico, one can see its peninsula, which was formed only recently by a volcanic eruption.

in the museum, then enjoy wine tastings and purchase your favorites from the shop. There is also a bar and restaurant, both with fine views over the coast. **Tacoronte**, nearby, is renowned for a much-venerated 17th-century figure of Christ. Known as the **Cristo de los Dolores** (Christ of Sorrows) it stands in the local church of the same name.

La Laguna, declared a World Heritage Site by UNESCO late in 1999, is Tenerife's second largest town and known as the ecclesiastic and cultural capital of the island. However, it is not well-visited by tourists. Start at the **Plaza del Adelantado**, and a short way along Calle Obispo Rey Redondo is the **cathedral** of La Laguna with its landmark twin bell towers. It is a surprisingly modern structure in spite of its design, consecrated in 1913, over 400 years after the city was founded. Continue on the same street to the town's oldest church, **Iglesia de Nuestra Señora de la Concepción** (Church of the Immaculate Conception), built in 1497. Its seven-story belfry and watchtower were added two centuries later. The interior is outstanding, with exquisite timber carvings on the ceiling and pulpit and an enormous Baroque altarpiece with Flemish panels.

West of Puerto

A full day's outing from Puerto de la Cruz along the unspoiled north and west coasts covers some of the island's most spectacular sights and scenery. Sleepy Icod de Los Vinos is the home of the botanical freak that is **Drago Milenario**, a 1,000-year-old Dragon Tree.

Continue west on the coast road from Icod to **Garachico** and after 6 km (3.7 miles) the tortuous descent begins. There are marvelous views looking directly down onto this compact little town of 6,000 inhabitants, set on a small peninsula with the waves crashing all around. The peninsula is actually formed from the volcanic debris that was deposited following a disastrous eruption in 1706, when most of the town and its inhabitants were destroyed. The best place to survey the aftermath of the petrified lava is from the beautifully preserved 16th-century **Castillo de San Miguel**. A lucky survivor, this fortress (note the heraldic arms above the doorway), is now devoted to handicraft sales. There is no beach to speak of here, but a very cleverly designed set of pools built into the rocks more than compensates. Despite the destruction, Garachico is a little gem. Neat houses boasting typically attractive Canarian balconies line cobbled streets, and old churches adorn pretty squares. Unmissable, also, is the large, uninhabited rock out in the bay, and it has managed to gain for itself a place in the spiritual life of

Garachico. Without a patron saint of its own, the town has elevated the rock to be its saint!

Farther along the coast road, 8 km (5 miles) past Buenavista del Norte, lies the most westerly point on Tenerife, the **Punta de Teno**. From here there are panoramic views across to La Gomera and looking south to the massive cliffs of Los Gigantes. Turn back to Buenavista and take a marked turn inland to Masca. Be warned, though, this is absolutely not a drive to be undertaken by inexperienced or nervous drivers. Initially the road, although ascending through the arable mountainside, is no problem; but this soon changes once the entrance to the vertiginous valley is reached. One glance at the narrow, steeply twisting road on either side will be enough to realize why, up to only a few years ago, the picturesque tiny village of **Masca** could only be reached on the back of a donkey. All around is some of the most dramatic scenery on the island. However, if you are driving, you won't have any time to savor it. The road clings precari-

The Magic of Manrique

César Manrique was Lanzarote's greatest artist, designer, landscaper, conservationist, and all-round cultural mandarin. Trained primarily in Madrid, he was born here in 1920 and died in 1992 in a car crash; there is hardly a visitor attraction that does not bear his signature in some way.

In his own words, his works were "dreams that capture the sublime natural beauty of Lanzarote," and he constantly strived to ensure that tourist developments were in harmony with the island's character. Simplicity was the key — whitewashed walls, natural building materials, classical or local music, and local food and wine are the Manrique hallmarks.

ously to the side of lush, green mountains cleft by deep, dark ravines and often zig-zags on itself in the tightest of hairpin bends. And it is far from unknown to have to reverse back down and around these bends, allowing other vehicles to pass. A stop at Masca is not just a pleasure, but also a relief. Relax at one of the restaurants down from the road, and enjoy the stupendous scenery before continuing south on an equally difficult drive, to rejoin the main road at Santiago del Teide.

A little farther south, turn off towards **Puerto de Santiago**, then walk out to the edge of the marina jetty to get the best view of the enormous sheer cliffs, up to 800 m (2,625 ft) high, known appropriately as **Los Gigantes** (The Giants).

The Central Area

There are several approaches to **Las Cañadas National Park** and **Mount Teide**. The park is well sign-posted from the road via La Orotava, but if you are coming from the north, then the most picturesque route is via **La Esperanza**. The small town soon gives way to a lush forest of giant pines and eucalyptus trees. Four km (2½ miles) south at Las Raíces is

Los Roques de Teide — a spectacular volcanic rock perched on a crater's edge.

where Franco met with his co-conspirators in 1936 (see page 20). An obelisk in the forest commemorates the event. As the road gains altitude and temperatures fall, the views become ever more spectacular. The Mirador Pico de las Flores looks out over to the southeast and the Mirador de Ortuño offers a panorama of the northern coast. Highest of all at over 2,000 m (6,562 ft), **Mirador las Cumbres** reveals Teide in all her glory.

The entrance to the National Park is **El Portillo de las Cañadas**, where there is a visitor center (open daily 9am–4pm). If you wish to walk in the park, pick up a leaflet or ask for information about the daily guided walks. Note that during winter the environment can become quite harsh, and you should never undertake walks without consulting staff at the visitor center first. At this point it is quite likely that you will be in the clouds; temperatures are very low, and in winter there may well be snow on the ground. The landscape becomes very lunar-like; it was around here that some of the filming for *Planet of the Apes* took place. The ascent to the top of Mount Teide can be made by climbing, or by the new **cable car** (*teleférico*), an eight-minute ride (open daily 9am–4pm, admission: 2,500 ptas, €15.03). Most visitors choose the cable car, but it's worth noting that even after leaving the cable car it is still a good climb

Painting by Sand

To celebrate the feast of Corpus Christi in May and June, detailed works of art are made by spreading multi-colored volcanic rock and sand particles on the ground in the same way that a conventional artist would spread paint onto a canvas. The Plaza Franco in front of the Palacio Municipal is the site for one such large-scale ground-stone artwork. Similar pictures are created with flowers both here and at La Laguna (see Festivals page 91).

to the summit at 3,717 m (12,195 ft). However, if you really want to venture that far you have to go in person and with a photocopy of your passport, to the Office of the Parque Nacional del Teide (Calle Emilio Calzadilla, 5, 38002 Santa Cruz de Tenerife). Even then, there is a daily limit of just 50 people, for conservation sake, allowed up the last 200 m (219 yards) to the summit. Once there, you should be able to count off all the other Canary Islands and, on a good day, see North Africa. Impressive as Teide is, it is basically no more than a peak on the edge of a giant volcano which long ago erupted or imploded. Left behind is the vast Caldera

The popular Playa Las Américas resort provides a good time for one and all.

(volcanic crater) which is most apparent from the area known as **Los Roques**. Los Roques are a group of giant, flamboyantly shaped lumps of volcanic rock rising out of the crater; often visited and photographed.

The East and South Coast

Candelaria is a town with deep religious roots. Legend has it that well before Christianity came to the Canaries an image of the Virgin was washed ashore here and worshipped by the Guanches, who were quite oblivious to its Christian significance. The Spaniards later built a church dedicated to the statue. Sadly, both the statue and the church were destroyed in 1826 when a tidal wave reclaimed the Virgin. The present over-sized **basilica** was built soon afterwards. The splendid new statue of Nuestra Señora de la Candelaria, the patron saint of the Canary Islands, is the object of a major pilgrimage in mid-August. The Guanches are not forgotten either: ten chieftains stand guard in a row, with their backs to the Atlantic. These idealized cavemen are truly noble savages.

Just south and inland from Candelaria is Güímar, which with the exception of one curiosity is easily overlooked. However, those with an interest in the history of these islands will be intrigued by the **Pirámides de Güímar** <www.fredolsen.es/piramides>. The step pyramids (also known as the Chacona pyramids) here didn't become evident until the early 1990s. They came to the notice of the Norwegian anthropologist Thor Heyerdahl, internationally acclaimed for his transoceanic crossings with prehistoric vessels and theories about human migration. After studying photos he came to the conclusion that the Chacona pyramids were similar in principal to those in the Old and New worlds. Subsequently, he took a personal interest and began to relate their existence to pre-Hispanic civilizations that either lived, or visited, the island. Today, on view, are not only the pyramids themselves, but models of Heyerdahl's vessels, a video detailing his summaries and transoceanic crossings, and various other interesting audio-visual displays.

There is little else of interest after here until you reach the south of the island. The most popular tourist destinations in Tenerife are the adjacent resorts of **Los Cristianos** and **Playa de las Américas**. Los Cristianos used to be a small fishing port with a quiet little beach. It now plays host to hundreds of thousands of mainly British and fewer German vacationers each year and its small beach, inside the port, is woefully inadequate. Traces of the old town can still be found around the port, though it is difficult to locate anything but British or German bars and restaurants along the crowded beachfront.

Playa de las Américas was born in the 1970s and has quickly developed from a bare shoreline to the high-rise, high-energy, highly packaged resort it is today. Here the beachside bars are not Spanish, nor even international: they are mainly

Date trees, a common sight in the Canary Islands, are easy to fall in love with.

English. In the evenings, of course, the hundreds of English bars compete with each other, some even advertising which British beers they sell on local English radio stations, for this lucrative and ever thirsty market. Discos, too, are ever popular with the younger crowd, but when they spill out in the early hours of the morning, good-natured boisterousness can sometimes result in rowdiness. Beware, also, of the dangers of muggings.

On the other side of Playa de las Américas, but with a border as indistinguishable as that with Los Cristianos, is the newly popular area of **Costa Adeje**, but here it really is rather different. The wall-to-wall hotels, fast food places and

To explore the ocean floor, take a trip on a yellow submarine. This beats an aquarium any day!

other such popular activities with the English and Germans gives way to much more elegant, spacious, cleverly designed resort hotels offering such extensive facilities that you don't even have to leave the property — creating a much more agreeable ambiance than that of its two near neighbors.

There is, of course, no shortage of entertainment facilities, and Puerto de Colón has become not just a favorite place to wander around and watch the boats, but a center for some really neat and unusual adventures that merit description. A submarine trip will appeal to most people and **Submarine Adventure** will take you under the ocean on a 45-minute trip in their yellow submarine. Through the picture windows you can monitor the progress, and the fish, yourselves. The highlight is when the submarine passes some wrecks on the sea bed which have become a haven for fish, notably an array of stingrays, some of which are frighteningly huge. **Safari B.O.B. Diving** has a more novel way of getting you underwater. B.O.B. stands for Breathing Observatory Bubble, and these are said to be the first in Europe. It is rather like a vertical scooter, and consists of a large bubble over your head and a steering apparatus by your waist. You get about 20 minutes of submerged time in the waters north of the port (open Monday–Thursday; Saturday.), and the cost is 6,500 ptas, €39.07 per person. **Speed Boat Safari, NautiOcio Watersports** is the latest, and fastest, water adventure; following an instructor you will drive your own boat exploring small bays and caves and stopping for swimming and snorkeling (all equipment provided: 10,000 ptas, €60.10 per person).

EL HIERRO

Area: 297 sq km (107 sq miles)
Population: 8,000

El Hierro has hardly any tourist facilities, no natural spectacles, and no good beaches, but it is pretty, quiet, and totally unspoiled. More than enough attributes, for many, to pay a visit. However, the configuration of the roads makes exploration a frustrating affair, as it is impossible to make a circular tour as roads just do not join up.

In the southwest corner of the archipelago El Hierro was, at one time, considered to be the end of the known world and for that reason it was used as the zero meridian, which has long since relocated to Greenwich.

Valverde

The only Canaries capital located inland, Valverde was built high on a mountainside to protect it from pirate raids, and is a very small town, with only a parador and a few other places offering tourist accommodation.

The Rest of the Island

From Valverde follow the road to Isora, a neat little village of well-tended gardens. There are three *miradors* to enjoy on the road to El Pinar. The name comes from the pinewood forests that in places make up a gentle rolling landscape of fields and trees reminiscent of northern Europe. As the road descends south the greenery eventually peters out into volcanic badlands, and at the tip of the island is the fishing port of La Restinga.

The switchback road down to Frontera passes fertile cultivated fields and the occasional disused *lagar* (winepress).

Although not a typical sandy beach, El Golfo, also known as the "Green Lagoon," has a most unique beauty.

The bell tower of the church here is something of an oddity, being divorced from its body and set on top of a small hill next to it. From a distance the tiny tower set against the massive cliff side seems terribly remote, but as you approach it the illusion disappears and the main road passes within feet of the church and tower. The cliffs here, and all along the stretch of north coast known as **El Golfo**, were once actually part of an immense volcanic crater. However, some 50,000 years ago one side of it slid, violently, into the sea, leaving behind a gigantic bay with a semi-circumference of 25 km (15.5 miles) and cliffs of up to 1,000 m (3,280 ft). Although the last eruption on the island was over 200 years ago El Hierro, actually, has the highest density of volcanoes in the archipelago. There are over 500 cones on the surface, with an additional 300 covered by lava flows.

The road west leads to the village of Sabinosa, and just south of here, though only accessible by a long journey, is the Ermita de los Reyes and the forest of **El Sabinal**. The forest is made up of juniper trees (*sabinosas*) which are incredibly and grotesquely twisted, stunted, gnarled, and, in some cases, almost bent double by the wind.

The **Mirador de la Peña**, 8 km (5 miles) west of Valverde, is the newest, the most impressive, and arguably the only real tourist attraction on the island. Those familiar with the work of César Manrique (see page 30) will not need an introduction. The views are marvelous and the restaurant is one of the best on the island.

LA GOMERA

Area: 372 sq km (146 sq miles) — the sixth largest island.
Population: 17,000

La Gomera is, indeed, a dramatic and rugged mountainous island. It has a coastline that is dominated by dramatic cliffs

— there are very few beaches, and the interior is full of vertiginous, mostly verdant, valleys that are often lined with narrow fields stepped into the sides of the mountains. For extra effect these valleys are more often than not covered by a ceiling of cloud, whisked in by the trade winds, which seem to perpetually hang over the island. In the center, there is the unusually dense growth of trees and fauna in what is the **Parque Nacional Garajonay** (open Tuesday–Sunday 9:30am–4:30pm). Less than 20 km (12½ miles) from north to south, this amazing island has been declared a Property of Humanity by UNESCO. In fact, a third of the island, 12,450 hectares (30,774 acres) has been designated into seventeen protected areas. Such terrain, though, makes for difficulty in getting around, and even the Romans, had they ventured this way, would have found their legendary ability to build straight roads put to an impossible test. In fact, almost nowhere on the island will you find a straight stretch of road, everywhere you go the roads twist and turn continually, often turning back on themselves in hairpin bends. Making driving even more complicated is the fact that the roads, although improving, are often of poor quality, and the directional signs leave much to be desired.

Just 40 minutes away from Tenerife, La Gomera nevertheless remains unspoiled and authentic, with its steep, green, terraced hills and tranquil valleys.

San Sebastián

Capital and main port of the island, this small town will always be important as the place where Columbus took leave of the known world on 6 September 1492, on the voyage which revealed the New World. The Columbiana starts in the main square. A pavement mosaic shows the route of Columbus's voyage, and next to the large tree is the Casa de

The road into Valle Gran Rey twists endlessly back and forth. When driving, always keep your eyes on the road.

Aduana (the old Customs House). According to folklore, Columbus drew water from the well here, took it to the New World, and used it to baptize America. Leading off the square, the **Calle del Medio** is the only street of any consequence in town and features more connections with the great navigator. The **Iglesia de la Asunción**, built between 1490–1510, looks and feels so old that you can easily imagine Columbus praying in a dark recess — as a plaque here tells us he did, in 1492. A little way up the street is the modest Casa Columbiana/Casa de Colón, which is supposedly where he stayed in La Gomera.

The North

The road from San Sebastián climbs steeply and the views soon become quite dizzying. The highest peak on La

Gomera, Alto de Garajonay is 1,487 m (4,878 ft) — this is no great height by Canaries standards, yet the island often gives the impression of being a fearsome maze of eerie crags. The small town of Hermigua is the largest on the island after San Sebastián. Stop at the crafts center of **Los Telares** to take a look down into its green and fertile valley, and ask if you can try the local liqueur, *mistela*, whilst watching women making blankets and rugs on their antique looms. After this there are fine views of the impressive cliffs, and Agulo is a pleasant small town whose main feature is the domed Iglesia San Marco, which adjoins a monumental laurel tree in the plaza. This church was originally a mosque during a brief period of Moorish occupation in the 17th century.

A turn inland just before the village of Las Rosas is one of the entrances to the **Garajonay National Park**, declared a World Heritage Site by UNESCO. The *Centro de Interpretación* (information center); has a small museum, displays and gardens. The road then continues through the 4,000-hectare (9,884-acre) park to the **La Laguna Grande** restaurant, a hospitable, rough-and-ready sort of place, which is very popular with walkers. Unlike the national parks at the peaks of many of the Canary Islands there are no views from here, aside from at Garajonay itself, and an almost perpetual thick mist clings to the ancient, moss-covered trees. As there is little rainfall on La Gomera this mist, spawned by the mystical trade winds, assumes great ecological importance having given life to this sub-tropical forest.

The South

The main road from San Sebastián leads past three mighty volcanic plugs, which are nicknamed "the Chinese Hat," "the Lion," and "the Face of Christ" after their respective

*The harbor in San Sebastián is a source of many legends,
some tracing all the way back to Columbus' times.*

outlines. The windy pass of **Degollada de Peraza** offers
spectacular views to both the north and the south, and the
road splits here. Rather than continue on to Garajonay,
turn left on an equally windy road that leads to **Playa
Santiago**. Besides San Sebastián this is one of the few
waterside communities on the island. The unpretentious
little port and beach is almost totally unspoiled by any out-
ward signs of tourism, even though the cliffs immediately
to its east are home to the *Jardín Tecina,* a really special
self-contained resort.

Continue inland, passing the new airport, and at Igualero turn
west onto the minor road that crosses to Las Hayas. Stop in the
small village of El Cercado where, almost next door to each
other, there are the *Rufina* and *Malria*, two small stores where

Beachgoers enjoy the black sand and hot sun at Playa Gran Rey.

the owners make ceramic goods in the traditional manner. Watch as little old ladies fashion the clay, and then be tempted to purchase the end results, or other goods and antiques that are on sale. Be surprised, also, by the prices; they are nearly as steep as the island's cliffs and valleys! From Las Hayas continue along to the main road at Arure where, immediately after turning left, there is a small bodega selling wines not only from La Gomera but from throughout the Canary Islands too. La Gomera actually has about 300 hectares (741.3 acres) of vineyards mostly cultivated on uneven land with steep slopes and small terraces. A stop at the highest point of this road is a must: The views from the combined mirador/restaurant Escuela César Manrique of the Valle Gran Rey (the multi-tiered valley not the town of the same name) below are stupendous. The small town of **Valle Gran Rey** even has a beach of some size, albeit of black sand, and accompanying restaurants. Follow the road back through the valley, continue on past Arure and then make a right at the T-junction with the other main road, and this leads all the way back to San Sebastián de La Gomera, passing La Laguna Grande and the entrance to Garajonay along the way.

LA PALMA

Area: 725 sq km (280 sq miles) — the fifth largest island.
Population: 81,500

La Palma, the most northwesterly of the Canaries, has two
nicknames — *La Isla Bonita* (the beautiful island) and *La
Isla Verde* (the green island), and both are suitable. Beautiful
it certainly is, and very green too. Not only that but its sta-
tistics are very impressive. The highest peak, Roque de los
Muchachos, rises 2,423 m (7,950 ft) above sea level, making
it the steepest island in the world in relation to its total area.
It is also the only one of the Canary Islands to have even very
small streams.

Santa Cruz de la Palma

The island capital is an appealing town — clean and bright
with traditional and modern architecture side-by-side creating much charm, especially when compared with many of
the other islands' rather bland capitals. The importance of
the town is such that, during the Renaissance era, it was the
third most important port of the Spanish Empire, after
Sevilla and Antwerp.

The heart of the town is the small triangular **Plaza de
España**, set a couple of streets in from the seafront on the
Calle Real. On one side of the triangle is the **Iglesia Matriz
de El Salvador** (Church of the Saviour), built in 1503. The
ceiling of this big stone church is made of *tea* (heart of pine)
and is a fine example of the Mudejar (Muslim under
Christian rule) style of intricate wooden paneling. Next to
the church are some splendid examples of 18th century colo-
nial-style mansions, notably the **Casa Monte Verde**, dating
from 1618 but having been rebuilt in 1922–1923. The
longest side of the triangle is taken up by the **ayuntamiento**
(Town Hall), built between 1559 and 1567 with stone

brought from La Gomera; this is considered the most important Renaissance building in the Canary Islands. While the arches are Italian Renaissance, the interior (which you are free to inspect) is Spanish colonial, with formidable carved wooden ceilings and doors, and a ceremonial staircase with frescoes painted by M. Cossío around 1950.

The **Calle Real** is a delightful street in which to stroll and enjoy the atmosphere. At its southern end it takes on the improbable title of Calle O'Daly, named after an Irish banana merchant who settled on the island. Look, also, on the parallel Avenida Maritimo at the wonderfully charming row of old houses known as the *Casas de los Balcones* Houses with balconies, built in the 19th century, they have become symbolic of Santa Cruz. Colorful and characteristic, and with a Portuguese influence, they have overhanging balconies, and those facing the sea were once used as lookout posts.

Due to the steep, dorsal shape of the island there are only two main island routes to follow: the loop south of the Caldera de Taburiente or the loop north of it. The southern route is the more interesting of the two.

The Southern Loop

Heading west from Santa Cruz the first stop of interest is **Las Nieves**, a village built on the mountainside. The first indica-

---

What's In A Name?

La Matanza, "the massacre," refers to a bloody Guanche victory at this site in 1494, when 900 Spanish troops were ambushed in a deep ravine. A year and a half later at nearby Acentejo, the Spanish exacted their revenge with interest, killing some 2,000 Guanches. *Victoria* (victory) was proclaimed and a chapel built in celebration. Within a few months the century-old Canaries campaign was over.

*Few can resist the stately charm that radiates from the
many terraces of the Casas de los Balcones.*

tion of it is a roadside bar, followed by the 17th-century
Santuario de Nuestra Señora de las Nieves (Sanctuary of
Our Lady of the Snows). This holds the venerated 14th-cen-
tury terracotta image of the Virgen de las Nieves, which
relates to an ancient miracle when the Virgin appeared in
Rome during August snow. Every five years the image is car-
ried to Santa Cruz in a procession known as *La Bajada de la
Virgen* (the Descent of the Virgin).

The next place of interest is the *Centro de Visitantes*
(Visitors Center) of the **Parque Nacional de la Caldera de**
Taburiente, located at Km 23.9 on road TF-812, (open daily
9am–2pm and 4pm–6:30pm). The English brochure is quite
helpful, giving general information on the geology and geo-

morphology, flora and fauna, helpful hints on camping as well as a very useful color diagram of the hiking possibilities. At the heart of La Palma, Caldera de Taburiente park, covering 4,690 hectares (just over 18 square miles), is a giant crater: 1,500 m (1,640 yards) deep with a diameter of 10 km (6.2 miles), and is a 20 km (12.4 miles) in circumference. It was created some 400,000 years ago and has since been colonized by nature into a green, fertile valley. The best place to see this is from the Mirador La Cumbrecita, which is 7 km (nearly 5 miles) away on the road next to the center. Following it, the road finally climbs into a craggy forest surrounded by mist-shrouded peaks with tall pines clinging to the most precarious ledges. There are wonderful views from here (weather per-

Hikers in a La Palma forest take full advantage of the natural beauty of this, "the green island."

mitting — which it doesn't most of the time), including the Roque de los Muchachos and the monolithic Roque Idafe, said to have been the sacred altar of the first Guanche natives on the island. You can enjoy the Caldera by car, but to get the most from the area you have to walk.

The main road then continues west through the city of Los Llanos de Aridane and then turns south, following the mountainside, to Fuencaliente. The most southerly point on the main road, it is famous for its wines. But rather than continue directly back north on the eastern side of La Palma, take the road down to the Faro de Fuencaliente that will lead you in a near circle to the most southern tip of La Palma and then up through a winding, twisting, road back to Fuencaliente. The first stop is at the **Bodegas Carballo**, where you can sample and purchase some surprisingly strong local wines. In 1677 the local volcano, San Antonio, erupted covering once fertile land with ash, leaving a layer of lapilli approximately 2 m (6.5 ft) deep. By the end of that century farmers had developed a technique of digging trenches that enabled them to reach the fertile layer of earth found under the cinders, where they planted the vines that were then covered with the extracted ashes. This somehow allowed the plants to resist adverse weather conditions and even the grape plague, *phylloxera*, that decimated vines all over Europe in the second half of the 19th century. Just across the road you can stop to pay a visit to the edge of the volcanic crater of **Volcán de San Antonio** and the mirador beyond it, (open daily 8am–6pm). In an exposed, windy location this looks, considering the damage it did, exceedingly benign. Just south of here are even more recent signs of volcanic activity; the volcano of **Teneguía** that erupted in 1971, fortunately without casualties. These eruptions sent an ever-widening stream of molten lava rushing down the green hillside here and you can see it now, petrified and black, as the road runs right through the once deadly mass. Surprisingly, *plátanos* (bananas) seem to take a liking to this environment, and can be seen thriving all around you. Once down to sea level you will come across the **Playa de Zamora** a small beach of jet-black sand squeezed in between the surrealistic lava fields. A short distance away, next to the twin lighthouses — one old and one new — is a tiny fishermen's cove with a stony beach that has a tiny restaurant, well, a shack really, that serves up the most delicious fresh fried fish (see page 139). After that there is nothing of note, except of course the lava fields and views, until you rejoin the main road at Fuencaliente.

Heading back north towards Santa Cruz, a stop at the Cueva de Belmaco is in order. Here, you will find the **Parque**

The Lady in the Tower

Why did Columbus choose Gomera to set sail from? Some say because it was the most westerly staging point known at that time, others point to a certain Beatriz de Bobadilla. Columbus certainly knew this Spanish beauty, and history indicates that she was quite free with her favors. You can ponder on this while contemplating the Torre del Conde (Tower of the Count) a little further on from the main square.

The Count in question, Hernán Peraza, the husband of Beatriz, was murdered one night at a mountain pass subsequently known at the Degollada de Peraza (the slaughter of Peraza). It seems that he had been leaving a native love nest and angry Guanches had ambushed him. Fearing an uprising by the local people, Beatriz retreated to the Tower and may well have entertained Columbus here. The building has not changed much in 500 years, although its present stranded site does leave much to be desired.

This panorama shows off the attractive parts of Santa Cruz de la Palma — the beach, the city, and the mountains.

Arqueológico de Belmaco (Archaeological Site of Belmaco). The first stone engravings found in the Canary Islands were discovered here in the 18th century, and the ten natural cave dwellings, with their magnificent rock engravings, were the home to the *Benahoritas* — the ancient settlers of *Benahoare*, the original aboriginal name for La Palma.

The Northern Loop

This is really of little interest, and the roads often leave something to be desired. However, a trip up the eastern coast from Santa Cruz to just south of Barlovento isn't too long, and the rather serpentine road runs through some pretty scenery. Make the first stop the **miradores** of **Bartolomé** and **La Montaña**, with the latter being a little higher and affording beautiful vistas along the coast in both directions. Head next for the seaside village of **San Andrés** and its natural swimming pools at *Charco Azul* (blue pool). A little inland from San Andrés and Sauces is the **Bosque de Los Tilos**, the largest wooded area in the whole Canary Islands and designated a "Biosphere Reserve" under the protection of UNESCO. Heritage of Mankind is the information center above the restaurant (open Monday–Friday 8am–3pm). The final destination though is a lovely, remote site just before Barlovento where, after a tortuously twisting journey down through banana plantations, you will reach the **Piscinas Fajana**; literally swimming pools built into the rocks and fed by the ocean waters that often crash into them. Showers and toilets are on hand, as is the pleasant *La Gaviota* (the Seagull), a restaurant/bar, and the views north of the cliffs falling straight into the ocean and being pounded by waves are breathtaking.

The goal in the north for most travelers is the **Roque de los Muchachos**, the highest point in the island at 2,423 m (7,950 ft) above sea level. There are several ways up to it, but always be aware of the weather; what looks fine from sea level takes on a different perspective at nearly 2,438 m (8,000 ft). And, of course, it can change dramatically and quickly, so go prepared clothes-wise, and know that you might not see much but clouds. Besides the views, the other attraction up here is the futuristic **Observatoria de Astrofísica**, regarded as the most important observatory in the Northern Hemisphere and home to some of the world's most important telescopes, including the 4-m (165-inch) William Herschel telescope. However, as it is only open to visitors for a few days each summer, most will have to be satisfied with just seeing it from the outside.

PROVINCE OF LAS PALMAS DE GRAN CANARIA:
Gran Canaria, Lanzarote and Fuerteventura (telephone code 928):

GRAN CANARIA

Area: 1,533 sq km (592 sq miles) — the third largest island.
Population: 715,000

Gran Canaria is second to none for its combination of perfect beaches and sophisticated nightlife, for its history and hubbub, marvelous natural scenery, sightseeing, and shopping. Almost circular in shape with a coastline of 236 km (over 146 miles), with over 50 km (31 miles) occupied by diverse beaches, Gran Canaria is the classic volcanic cone in profile, and its mountainous character causes the climate to change radically with latitude and altitude. You can leave a wet and chilly Las Palmas in the morning and an hour later be enjoying a hot, sunny day in Maspalomas.

Gran Canaria is known, not without reason, as the "continent in miniature." The coastline ranges from awe-inspiring cliffs to golden dunes. Inland you can choose between stark mountains and tranquil valleys; in fact, there are 32 protected areas that cover 42.7% of the island's surface.

La Playa de las Canteras — considered by many the Canaries' prettiest beach.

Las Palmas

Bustling Las Palmas, (population 450,000 — the largest city in the Canaries and the seventh largest in Spain), is a major commercial and historical center, a cosmopolitan resort, and a vital seaport all rolled into one. It is one of the busiest ports in the world.

The real hub of Las Palmas is the **Parque de Santa Catalina**. This square is effectively one gigantic outdoor café that buzzes day and night, and is just a short walk to **Playa de las Canteras.** This superb golden beach stretches for 3 to 5 km (2 to 3 miles) and a natural reef just offshore means that the water couldn't be calmer. Las Canteras and the area behind it reflect the city's cosmopolitan nature. Like the city in general, it has seen better days and is losing younger tourist trade to the smarter modern resorts in the south.

Away from Las Canteras make your first stop **Doramas Parque**, a pleasantly landscaped park named after a Guanche island chieftain, and adjacent to the park is the **Pueblo Canario** (Canary Village). This is a romanticized version of a Canarian village where you can shop for handicrafts and watch displays of folk dancing and singing. The man who conceived it was local artist and designer Néstor de la Torre (1888–1938), and a museum of his exotic art is in the Pueblo.

Further south is **Triana**, one of the older *barrios* (suburbs). Today it is known for its upmarket shops, and the long, pleasant, pedestrianized street of Calle Mayor de Triana offers just about everything for both tourists and locals. Adjoining Triana is **Vegueta**, the oldest part of the city, where Spanish forces first set up camp in 1478. History lurks behind every wall and this is a delightful place just to wander around.

*The buildings of Las Palmas present a veritable
Easter basket of calming pastel hues.*

Christopher Columbus knew these streets, and he prayed
at the **Ermita de San Antonio Abad** before setting off on
his first Voyage of Discovery to the New World. The present
building dates from the 18th century. Close by on Calle
Colón is the beautiful 15th-century **Casa de Colón**; this elegant house with its charming courtyard was formerly the residence of the island's first governor, and Columbus is said to
have stayed here on three occasions. Now an atmospheric
museum, it recreates the Age of Discovery with exhibits of
navigational instruments, charts, weapons, and everyday
items of the period.

Around the corner stands the vast Gothic and neo-Classic
bulk of the **Catedral de Santa Ana**, with its Diocesan
Museum of Sacred Art, which is not pretty but certainly
impressive, and best seen by night when floodlighting soft-
ens its harsh, grimy front. Facing the cathedral are several

green bronze statues of the aboriginal mastiff dogs after whom the Canary Islands are said to have been named (from the Latin *canes*).

Just down from the cathedral is the modernistic **Centro Atlantico de Arte Moderno (CAAM);** (Atlantic Center of Modern Art). With five floors of exhibitions, this is the southernmost contemporary art center in the European Union and focuses on the work of young Canarian creators. Nearby the **Museo Canario** holds the islands' most important collection from Guanche times, with the highlight being the room of skulls and mummies, depicting the Guanches' fascination with death (see page 14).

The hills surrounding here, and on the southern approach to Las Palmas, are full of apartment buildings and the like, and would not normally merit any attention. However, the city government readily realized that these areas looked, at the very least, rather bland. To counteract this they had the ingenuity to brighten them up; and nowadays all the buildings are painted in the most unusual, and very attractive, array of pastel colors.

Southern Exposure

The southern resorts of San Agustín, Playa del Inglés, and Maspalomas, the biggest holiday complex in all of Spain, let alone the Canaries, are linked to Las Palmas and Gran Canaria international airport by the fast and featureless *autopista* (motorway).

San Agustín is a restrained area of apartments, catering for more mature and discerning vacationers. **Playa del Inglés** is more robust, as the very name (Beach of the English) might suggest, although it attracts numerous German visitors as well. This is a fun-and-sun sprawling resort of high-rise hotels, shopping malls, and fast-food restaurants. The nightlife at the more than numerous discos, bars and clubs can be hectic. During the day people can sun themselves on the golden beaches that stretch for 16 featureless kilometers (10 miles), so there is room enough for everyone. **Maspalomas** is famous for its **dunes** that cover an wide area of 250 hectares (618 acres), which are sufficiently large and unspoiled to constitute a mini-Sahara of great beauty. They are a protected nature reserve, but you are far more likely to see naturists than naturalists here. Playa de Maspalomas is the stretch of dunes close to the landmark

A desolate trek — hikers traverse the dunes at Maspalomas, on Gran Canaria.

lighthouse and is home to a small, but ever growing, number of top-class hotels.

As you might expect, there is the usual plethora of family attractions nearby, the most important of which is **Palmitos Parque,** that provides an excellent day out for all the family. Performing parrots amuse with circus tricks, and caged birds of every imaginable hue are kept in beautiful gardens. The real stars, however, are the exotic free-flying residents. **AquaSur** is, at 130,000 square m (over 32 acres), the largest waterpark in the Canary Islands. The other major attraction, **Sioux City,** is a recreation of the Wild West, with gun-fights, lynchings, saloon gals and lassooing tricks, etc.

The Friday evening Big Wild West Show (with barbecue) is great fun for children.

West of Maspalomas the coastline becomes dominated by towering, rather barren looking cliffs, that every now and again form natural bays and coves well-suited to become resorts in their own right. However, this area is overdeveloped; what is surprising is that development continues apace, especially given the lack of building space. Developers, however, have resolved this problem very innovatively by literally building into the cliff sides themselves, and this often leaves visitors with the rather surreal sight of wall-to-wall development taking up every inch of these steep bays. Nevertheless, some of the places retain a certain charm.

Puerto Rico is the most attractive beach resort on this coast. But it too has been grossly overdeveloped, so its lovely, sheltered, golden beach can become unbearably crowded. Its marina is the focal point for numerous marine adventures that will

suit all tastes. **Líneas Salmón** has eight boats and runs a frequent and inexpensive ferry service between Puerto Rico, Arguineguín and Mogán, offering a charming way of getting to know this part of the coastline. **Afriyachts, Puerto Rico** has two catamarans that run five-hour cruises. Dolphin cruises are popular too, and glass bottom boats operate

The resort at Puerto Rico is equipped to cater to a wide array of tastes.

from the port. Sport fishing will appeal to the more adventurous, and this part of the coast is just the place for it; consequently, numerous boats operate from Puerto Rico.

Puerto de Mogán should be a lesson to all resort developers in how to provide accommodation that is functional, very attractive and totally in sympathy with its surroundings. The accommodation here is an interpretation of local townhouses that are ablaze with bougainvillea, arranged in pedestrian-only squares with narrow alleyways and arches leading to an attractive marina. This is lined with stylish cafés and restaurants, jazz and piano bars, and small boutiques. All that is lacking is a good beach. A submarine trip also dives from here, and one of the best nautical trips is an excursion aboard the **Windjammer San Miguel,** a fine old transatlantic sailing ship built in 1919.

Northern Coast and Hinterland

Arucas, is a workaday town overshadowed by an immense 20th-century neo-Gothic cathedral that stands out like a sore thumb. The road west from Arucas follows a truly dizzying route through the mountains past several caves. Some provide shelter for goats, but others are inhabited by people and are complete with running water and electricity. The route passes through the tidy small town of **Moya**. It is well worth stopping to see its church, precariously perched on the very edge of a ravine. An act of faith indeed!

Just off the coast road is the **Cenobio de Valerón** (Convent of Valerón). This is badly sign-posted. Take the turn off just before Guía, away from the sea. This convent is actually a series of Guanche caves cut into a steep mountainside. According to island lore, the daughters of noble families spent their youth in these small cells serving the native gods. At the age of 15 they were allowed to marry or to remain in the sanctuary for life. More prosaically, the caves were probably also used for grain storage. Around this area, you could spy some modern cave dwellers.

Continue south towards **Agaete**, which is the most attractive of the small northern towns. Agaete's port, **Puerto de las Nieves,** is a haven of calm among the formidable rocky cliffs that make up this inhospitable stretch of coast. From here the coast road ascends very sharply amid sparse, wind-blown greenery, and the drop seawards can be frighteningly steep. An alternative route is to drive 7 km (4 miles) inland to the fine viewpoint at **Los Berrazales**.

Central Sights

The mountainous center of the island makes for very tiring driving. You will rarely get out of the lower gears, but the wonderful panoramas are ample reward. Pine forests, almond groves, gnarled mountains, sheer cliffs, and cloudy mountaintops beckon.

Whistle Down The Wind

The problem of being so close and yet so far, and how to communicate across the hilltops, was solved a long time before the telephone came to Gomera. For ages, gossip and messages have been transmitted across the ravines by the language of *el silbo* (the whistle). This is a real language of regulated tones and rhythms representing words, whistled with or without the aid of fingers in the mouth, at great volume. Only a small minority of Gomerans keep the language alive. Many younger people may understand it, but they cannot converse in *silbo*. If you do not go on a coach tour that takes you to see *silbo* in action, try Las Rosas restaurant at the village of the same name, or the parador at San Sebastián, where the gardeners may be able to oblige you.

The best and certainly the most popular vantage point is the **Cruz de Tejeda** (Cross of Tejeda) — at 1,463 m (4,800 ft), one of the few points inland where you are almost guaranteed to meet fellow tourists. A small cluster of cafés, fruit and souvenir stalls, and men with donkeys await you at the summit. The magnificent panorama includes two rock formations that were once worshipped by the Guanches. The most distinctive is the statuesque, dark, broody bulk of **Roque Nublo** at 1,817 m (5,961 ft), and it takes little imagination to understand the primitive inhabitants' fascination with

Hello there! A man and his donkey provide a warm welcome at the Cross of Tejada.

this formation; the other is the Roque Bentaiga.

As the Cruz de Tejeda is the hub of the island, there are any number of routes to and from it and almost all have something to offer, so consider ascending on one route and descending via another.

From Las Palmas you have two options. The most northern route runs through the peaceful valley town of **Teror**. The old whitewashed houses, often built around graceful patios, boast fine traditional carved balconies. The major landmark here is a typically large Canarian church, the **Basílica Nuestra Señora del Pino** (Our Lady of the Pine). This commemorates the miraculous discovery in 1481, in the branches of a pine tree, of a sacred effigy. The Blessed Virgin of Teror is also the patron saint of Gran Canaria. Alternatively, take the main road that runs inland from close to the cathedral and heads southwest through the towns of Santa Brígida and Vega de San Mateo, offering panoramic views of the east of the island. Because the climate here is exceptionally mild, many Canarians and foreign residents have built very desirable homes in these hills, with the gardens around their villas often being magnificent. A small diversion along this route is certainly worthwhile. Just a few kilometers out of Las Palmas, follow the signs to Bandama, the road (open 8am–10pm) leads up to the nearby **Caldera de Bandama**, one of the island's finest natural features and a spectacular mirador in its own right. This volcanic crater, almost a kilometer (more than a half mile) across, is green, fertile.and drops some 198 m (650 ft) down. A scenic spiraling road leads to the top, where the Real Club de Golf enjoys such a picturesque location that even non-golfers are tempted to pick up a club. The views from here take in the mountains, fertile valley and vast stretches of the coastline from Las Palmas to the distant south.

From the west of the island drive north from Agaete and then turn inland following the signs to Tejeda for a really pleasant, and not unduly difficult, mountain ascent. The valleys here are wide and their slopes play host to some small farms; it is one of the few places in the islands where you will come across farm animals. Of interest, too, are the fantastic views across the ocean on a fine day to the snow-capped Mount Teide floating majestically above the clouds and the mountain peaks and lush valleys of Gran Canaria itself. Before reaching Tejeda turn off to the village of Artenara, to the southwest, and what is undoubtedly the best restaurant view on the island. The place in question is

These volcanic formations, once worshipped by the Guanches, still inspire wonder and awe in intrepid travelers.

Méson de la Silla, not easy to spot, parallel to the main road. A dark tunnel leads through the rock with no hint of what is to come, then emerges on the other side of the mountain to a bright 180-degree mountain panorama. To the left the head of the valley, green and dotted with white-washed little villages; it leads up to Tejeda itself, but the more dramatic vistas are directly in front and to the right. Here, the scenario is dramatic indeed; jagged peaks fill the horizon and many smaller ones are spread throughout the valley giving the impression of looking down on a minor mountain range.

LANZAROTE

Area: 803 sq km (310 sq miles) — the fourth largest island.
Population: 77,000

Lanzarote is a startling place, representing the triumph of civilization over a hostile environment, and the entire island has been declared a Biosphere Reserve by UNESCO. Its pock-marked, lunar-like surface, 60 km (37 miles) long and 20 km (12 1/2 miles) wide, is dotted with more than 300 volcanoes, yet onions, potatoes, tomatoes, melons, and grapes all spring in abundance from the black ash. Its most unusual farm crop, however, is the Cochineal Beetle that, when squashed, emits a red dye used as coloring for Campari and lipsticks. Newer to the tourist scene than either Gran Canaria or Tenerife, Lanzarote seems to have learned from the excesses of its sister islands. Here, small is beautiful and harmony with the environment is the philosophy.

The South of the Island

Arrecife, the principal port and latter-day capital is a characterless place with just two saving graces — the Castillo de San Gabriel and the Castillo de San José. The 16th-century **Castillo de San**

The Castillo de San José — inside this old fortress is a modern art museum.

Gabriel, situated close to the center of town, houses a small museum of no great standing. But it is worth the walk across the small drawbridge and over the lagoon, onto the small island that the castle used to deter pirates. The **Castillo de San José,** a few kilometers, to the north, is a far more interesting proposition. Built in the 18th century, this well-preserved fortress that once guarded the harbor it overlooks, now houses the late César Manrique's small but impressive **International Museum of Contemporary Art**. This includes works by Picasso and Miró, and is also notable for the contrast between the modern exhibits and the ancient structure that houses them.

The island's major resort is **Puerto del Carmen** and its long golden beach stretches for about 5 km (3 miles) and comfortably accommodates its visitors. The sea is calm and ideal for families. Restaurants of every conceivable type, bars, and shops line the Avenida de las Playas, Lanzarote's one outbreak of mass commercialism.

The **old town** just west of the beach has a charming small harbor area with traditional bars and restaurants and an array of marine adventures awaiting you. Of these, the **Blue Delfin** and the **Princesa Ico**, both glass bottomed catamarans, offer a variety of trips, sport fishing charters leave from here also. If you prefer seeing the area from the air, albeit attached to a motorboat, then **Paracraft** offers you the chance to paraglide.

The road west leads through the beautifully tended village of to the rather more earthy **Salinas de Janubio** (Salt Flats at Janubio). Every spring, for the Corpus Christi festivities, the flats provide the salt that local artists dye into a variety of colors and pour onto the streets of Arrecife to create religious and secular designs (see page 32). A little farther north are two more natural spectacles. **Los Hervideros** is a section of rocky coast where the crashing waves break

These roses in the garden-like village of Yaiza are growing in volcanic topsoil that acts as a sponge in the night air.

ferociously against the cliffs and sea caves. **El Golfo**, by contrast, is a placid, emerald-green lagoon set beside a cliff that resembles a gigantic petrified tidal wave just about to break. This is actually the inner rim of a volcanic cone, half of which has disappeared beneath the sea. The strata, colors, and manic whirls are a fascinating sight. Note that El Golfo is not apparent from the roadside. Park your car on the rough ledge, just off the main road on the left as you begin the descent into the village of El Golfo (renowned for the quality of its fish restaurants), and follow the rough footpath over the cliff.

The newly created resort of **Playa Blanca** on the south coast, the third major tourist center on the island, is host to the Fuerteventura ferry, a marina and a good golden beach.

However, just a few miles east along unpaved roads are the best sands on the island, collectively known as the **Papagayo (parrot) beaches**. You will need a four-wheel-drive vehicle, local directions (there are no signposts), and little else, as on Papagayo naturism is the norm. The **Ganges Seis** is a taxi boat that will drop you off there in the morning and return to pick you up in the afternoon. An alternate way to get there is to take the **Catlanza s.l.** a modern catamaran that sails out of Puerto Calero — the highlight is when it drops anchor 46 m (50 yards) off the Papagayo beach.

Puerto Calero, just a few minutes south of Puerto del Carmen, but with an entirely different ambiance, is a rather new and dominated by its modern marina that is lined by a row of restaurants offering all kinds of cuisine. Besides the Catlanza catamaran it is also the home port of **Submarine Safaris** which offers the opportunity to explore under the local waters. The trip that lasts one hour, and when it settles onto the seabed 30 m (33 yards) or so down, divers go out to feed the fish.

The highlight of your trip to Lanzarote and the magical ingredient that makes this island so special is to be found in the **Montañas del Fuego** (Mountains of Fire). The Parque Nacional de Timanfaya, which encompasses the mountains in its 200 square km (77.2 square miles), starts just north of Yaiza, and its boundary is marked by an impish devil motif. This desolate national park was formed largely over the course of 16 cataclysmic months during 1730 and 1731. Eleven villages were buried forever and many of the people left the island for Gran Canaria.

Drive on and turn left at the small roundabout to the Montañas del Fuego. Your introduction to the inner sanctum of the mountains leaves no doubt that at least one of these volcanoes (in fact the very one that you are standing on!) is not dead, just sleeping. In fact, less than 10 m (32 ft) under the surface the temperature reaches as much as 600° C (1,112°F), and at the surface level it can, at certain places, get to 120° C (248°F). A guide demonstrates this by pouring water down a tube into the earth, then beating a hasty retreat. Seconds later a geyser erupts, startling the diners in the adjacent restaurant.

Cars are not allowed any farther into the park, and from here coach tours — included in the admission price, depart to explore the incredible landscape. Any badlands that you may have seen up to this point have been a mere appetizer for the main course. The words *lunar* and *alien* are worked to exhaustion in attempts to describe the area, and still scarcely do justice to the dramatic scenery. This was caused by a massive eruption (the volcano was active from September 1730 to April 1736), during which 420 houses were completely destroyed. The last activity of the volcano began in 1824 and lasted 10 years.

This bodega is one of several in the La Geria valley where visitors can sample the local wine and sherry.

With rain so rare and underground water sources extremely limited you may wonder how Lanzarote manages to survive as an agricultural island. The black topsoil is the secret, discovered by the farmers in their adversity. The porous volcanic particles that make up the topsoil are useless in themselves but act as a sponge for the moisture of the night air, obtaining water for the plants and eliminating the need for rain. They are therefore piled on top of the crops and only need replacing around once every 20 years. The other Canary Islands also use this method.

The most impressive example of this type of farming is the vineyards around the valley of **La Geria**. Each vine is set in its own mini-crater, protected from wind and excess sun by a low semi-circular wall of lava stones (other crops are also protected in this manner). The horseshoe patterns thus formed stretch way up the mountains and apparently into infinity, producing an almost hypnotic effect. Not only do the vineyards look good, the end product also tastes very good, and there are several *bodegas* in the Geria valley where you can sample the excellent local *malvasía*. Those with an interest in wine will want to pay a visit to the **Museo del Vino de Lanzarote, El Grifo;** not too far away at San Bartolomé de Lanzarote. The Monument to El Grifo, a Manrique creation, adorns the entrance to this bodega that has been producing wines since the 18th century. It is the oldest in the Canaries. Enjoy the exhibitions of wine-making tools, stroll through the vineyards and, of course, partake of the wine tasting sessions.

The North of the Island

On an island so dominated by the works and creativity of one man, it would be inappropriate not to pay a visit to the **Fundación César Manrique**; Taro de Tahíche; Manrique lived here and, as you might have come to expect, it is rather unusual. Built in 1968, it is located over a river of lava formed from the eruptions between 1730 and 1736 and takes advantage, at its lowest point, of five volcanic bubbles to create the strange, but nonetheless impressive living space.

The geographic center of Lanzarote lies 9 km (5½ miles) northwest of the capital at Mozaga, focal point of the island's viniculture. Here the late César Manrique designed and erected a huge white modern sculpture, **Monumento al Campesino**, dedicated to the peasant workers of the island.

A few miles north of La Santa, home to the Club La Santa a time-share development resort where athletes of the highest level come for both training and relaxation, is the tiny village of Caleta de Famara. It has windswept beaches with views of the daunting cliffs of the Famara Massif that lead up to the Mirador del Río and Graciosa island. There is not much to do along this coastline except sunbathe and windsurf, but as the currents can be dangerous here, be sure to take care.

Burglary at the Basilica

On 17 January 1975, the richly robed, bejeweled, and crowned statue of Madonna and Child was the target of one of the most sensational (and professional) crimes in Canaries' history. Burglars broke through the 200-year-old ceiling of the church and stripped the most important diamonds, sapphires, and gold and silver votive adornments from the statue. They left behind many items considered less valuable — or impossible to dispose of. Estimates on the haul range from 10–20 million pesetas.

For a small charge you can enter the treasury of the church and see the statue of the patron saint on her silver throne. Buy a pre-robbery postcard and you will have some idea of just how much jewelry was taken.

Local merchants and shoppers come together for the Sunday market in the town center of Tequise.

Teguise is a fine old town of cobbled streets and gracious mansions and was the island capital until 1852. Now it is calm and quiet for six days of the week. On Sundays a **handicrafts market** comes to town where you can buy a *timple* — a small ukulele-like instrument used by local folkloric musicians. Several of its old buildings have been converted to craft and antique shops and restaurants. Overlooking the town is the 16th-century **Castillo de Santa Bárbara**. The views from this wind-blown point are worth the trip alone. High on top of the extinct volcano of Guanapay, the castle now hosts the **Museo del Emigrante Canario**, where sepia photos and nostalgic exhibits tell the sad story of how mass emigration to South America was the only option left for many Canarian families.

Costa Teguise, just north of Arrecife, is a totally modern resort, comprising several *urbanizaciónes* with time-shares, ho-

This windmill and cactus garden is but one of Cesar Manrique's landscapes.

tels, and apartments designed for a wealthy clientele. It is no surprise to realize that the King and Queen of Spain have an official residence here, and it is where they welcomed the New Milennium. There is a handful of good sandy beaches, particularly Playa de las Cucharas, where water sports thrive and windsurfing is particularly popular. Look for the championship golf course and the **Ocean Park Water Park**.

The coast road east passes the town of Guatiza, where prickly pears abound and where cochineal beetles are still cultivated (see page 19). César Manrique also cultivated the spiny flora into a beautiful **Jardín de Cactus** complete with a working windmill that produces its own *gofio* (see page 15). There is more Manrique design to admire at the caves of **Jameos del Agua**; opened in 1966, this was the first attraction designed by the great creator, where his landscaping talents have embellished and transformed a grotto and underground lagoon into a short fantasy journey. Ethereal mood music accompanies your descent into the cave, lushly planted with luxuriant foliage. Peer into the black lagoon and you can pick out the very rare, tiny blind albino crabs, *Munidopsis poly-*

morpha, which live here. Resist, though, the temptation to throw coins into the crystal clear lagoon; the attendant corrosion of the metal kills the crabs. Finally you emerge from the cave into a South Seas paradise, complete with its accompanying swimming pool. In the evening the Jameos del Agua is transformed into a night-club where folklore shows are regularly staged. The **Cueva de los Verdes** (Green Caves) found a short distance away across the main road, are part of the same system, and were blasted through the earth by exploding lava. There is a guided tour that includes some memorable sound and light effects, evoking the menacing volcano most effectively.

At the northern tip of the island is the small fishing port of **Orzola**. This is the embarkation point for the tiny island of **Graciosa**, a ferry service run by **Líneas Maritimas Romero** four times a day (July–Sep) and three times the rest of the year. With superb beaches and a complete lack of tourist development, this is the place to get away from it all for the day.

For an unforgettable view of **Isla Graciosa** and much more, drive up to the **Mirador del Río** (admission: 400 ptas, €2.40). This is yet another of César Manrique's creations, and one that certainly shouldn't be missed. The views from here really are wonderful indeed, and it is probably the most spectacular *mirador* in all the Canaries. Huge cliffs curve down to the beach with Graciosa just across the water and with the two other smaller islands, Montaña Clara and Alegranza, in the background. Combined with Graciosa and a small section of the northwest coastline of Lanzarote, they form the *Parque Nacional del Archipiélago Chinijo*. The only sound here is that of the wind gently whistling through *El Río*, the waterway separating Lanzarote and Graciosa. Besides its huge picture windows, note in the bar/restaurant some more of Manrique's creative sculptures.

Another addition to the island's burgeoning tourist attractions is the **Guinate Tropical Bird Park,** just south of the Mirador del Río. Within its 45,000 square m (11.1 acres) of carefully tended landscaped gardens you will find over 1,300 species of rare and exotic birds and animals, a new area where you can discover the world of Tamarind monkeys, and of course, performing parrots entertain in the theatre.

FUERTEVENTURA

Area: 2,020 sq km (780 sq miles) — the second largest island.
Population: 42,000

Beaches on Fuerteventura still outnumber hotels. At the last count there were 152 beaches along the 340 km (210 miles) of coastline; 50 km (31 miles) of which are of yellow sand and 25 km (16 miles) of black sand and stone, giving it the best selection of beaches in the Canary Islands. Enhancing these even more, Fuerteventura's coastal shelf allows for the existence of shallow transparent waters that often acquire a beautiful turquoise color. The island is situated less than 115 km (71 miles) off the coast of North Africa, and most of its sand is blown here from the Sahara, giving a new meaning to the term "desert island."

A windsurfer enjoys the near-perfect conditions at Corralejo beach.

Fuerteventura is barren and windswept almost to the point of desolation — or grandeur, depending on your point of view. So sparse is the population that the density, 22 inhabitants per square km, is the lowest of the islands. Goats survive better here than people and they outnumber the human inhabitants. However, the harsh terrain can only support so many goats. The females survive for their milk and famous Majorero cheese, Blanco (white) or Rojo (red) according to the color of the crust. A few lucky males are kept for breeding purposes but the rest are destined for the dinner table.

The wind whistles with great force in Fuerteventura and may even have given the island its name, a corruption and inversion of *el viento fuerte* (the strong wind). However, it is a wind that seems to be bringing good fortune to the island, as the presence of so many windsurfers proves. With the growth of tourism the island has become one of the world's leading windsurfing centers.

The North

The once sleepy fishing port of **Corralejo** has been transformed into the busy Lanzarote ferry terminal and a bustling resort popular with the British. Although the old port area still has colorful fishing boats and some good fish restaurants the town is, in the main, somewhat less than inspiring and one of the least pleasant of the resorts in the Canary Islands favored by the British.

There are two routes south to Puerto del Rosario, the capital. FV-1 follows the east coast of the island, and just a few minutes from the center of Corralejo there are some magnificent, long white beaches and dunes stretching for some 30 square km (12 square miles). These, (along with **Isla de los Lobos**), have been declared a national park and are popular with nudists. The island lies 3 km (2 miles) offshore, and its beaches are even more secluded than those on the "mainland." The fishing here

Fuerteventura is home to old craft traditions, such as lace-making.

is outstanding. Glass-bottomed ferry-boats depart regularly from Corralejo. The rest of the route to Puerto del Rosario, once named Puerto Cabras (Port of the Goats) because in the 18th century it was used mainly for the raising of goats, has nothing of interest for tourists and the town itself is a rather drab place.

The inland route south to Puerto del Rosario follows the FV-101 and a diversion, west along the FV-109 will bring you first to the **Zoo Safari Calderón Hondo.** There you can opt for either a half-hour camel trip or a 1½ hour safari to the lunar landscape of the Volcano Calderón Hondo. Next comes the lace-making town of Lajares. And if you really want to get away from it all, continue on to **El Cotillo**. This tiny fishing village on the east coast also boasts some excellent beaches wonderful for windsurfing, plus a handful of local bars and some basic restaurants. Heading back south from El Cotillo, the FV-10 rejoins the FV-101 at the small town of **La Oliva**. This is not especially attractive but it does feature two places of interest. Just off the main road stands the Casa de los Coroneles (House of the Colonels). Its name derives from its 18th-century tenants who once ruled the island. The decaying, cream-colored building still exudes a certain haughty, if melancholy, grandeur. By contrast, the nearby Centro de Arte Canario is bright and modern, exhibiting the works of some of the finest living Canarian artists.

A little further south, just past Tindaya, the road makes a dog-leg towards Puerto in the east, and if you look very carefully to your right you will see, at the base of one of the mountains, the **Monumento a Don Miguel de Unamuno**. Unamuno, a writer and vice-chancellor of the famous University of Salamanca, the oldest in Spain, made himself unpopular in 1924 with the dictator of Spain, General Primo de Ribera. His criticisms of the dictator resulted in his being exiled to Fuerteventura. Although he fled to the somewhat more civilized Paris after a few months, he loved to describe the beauty of the islands in his writing. His most famous quote states that the Canaries were "an oasis in the desert of civilization."

The Central Area

The central mountain range is encircled by two roads: the FV-20 that initially heads west from Puerto del Rosario then drops south alongside the mountains to Antigua and Tuineje before meeting up with the main north to south FV-2 just north of Gran Tarajal; and the FV-30 that loops around, off the FV-20 north of the range, dropping into the Betancuria valley and continuing south through winding terrain to Pájara and Tuinije, where it meets up again with the FV-20. As you can join this loop from the north, south or center, and even cut across the mountains at one point, you can start out from most parts of the island. Starting from Puerto del Rosario take the FV-30 diversion off the FV-20 and follow it until you see the signs for the **Mirador de Morro Velosa**; soon a gate man will demand 300 ptas, €1.80 per person, but this will prove to be a worthwhile investment. At the summit and with commanding views of the surrounding mountains and with the Atlantic Ocean shimmering in the distance, is a delightful combination of café, bar and viewpoint that owes its creative design to none other than César Manrique.

Betancuria, by far the most attractive and visited inland town on the island, is an oasis of greenery on this barren island. Although the riverbed here is almost perpetually dry, the town is fortunate to have a high water table. Because of its theoretical invulnerability at the heart of the island, it was made Fuerteventura's first capital in the early 15th century. However, in 1539 somehow the ravaging Berber pirates overcame the mountains (which still provide a difficult drive today), and destroyed the original cathedral. The present 17th-century church, **Iglesia de Santa María** is a splendid building and hosts many interesting treasures. Look at the unusual wooden beams between the flagstones on the floor, the wooden altar and choir, and the decorated pulpit. Adjacent to the museum is a leather factory-cum-shoe-shop, set in an atmospheric old building. Wander round this lovely little town and admire the view from across the bridge, where there is an unpretentious restaurant/bar and a gift shop. Just south of Betancuria is the neat and pretty village of **Pájara**, but a stop at Antigua, on the other side of the mountains is in order. This is reached either by continuing on the loop past Tuineje, or backtracking from Betancuria and taking the FV-416 across the mountains. In either event, once in Antigua — the island's capital from 1834–1835 — you can't miss the traditional old windmill found just to the north of town, and this is your destination. Actually, the **Centro de Artesania "Molino de Antigua"** (Windmill Crafts Center) is much more than just that, and has something for almost everyone's tastes. Interesting crafts and a visit inside the windmill certainly, but also ethnographic and archaeological exhibitions, modern art, an audio-visual room, rooftop viewpoints and an intriguing cactus garden, not to mention a nice restaurant.

Of the coastline south of Puerto del Rosario, the new cosmopolitan development of **El Castillo**, also known as **Caleta de Fuste**, is of most interest. Activities here focus around the attractive, horse-shoe-shaped beach (where windsurfing is a particularly popular sport), and the well-designed marina. In the marina, there is an area where you can view the fish that frequent its waters, and a small number of activities use the harbor as a home-port. The **Oceanarium** is a

The greenery of Betancuria stands in contrast to the rest of arid Fuerteventura.

catamaran that will take you out to visit the dolphins and whales, and the **Nautilus** is a semi-submersible submarine that has twenty individual seats.

The South

The main attraction is the 26-km- (16-mile-) long sandy shores of **Jandía** that run from the narrowest part of Fuerteventura down to Morro Jable. At the northern tip of the Jandía sands are the beautiful beaches of **Costa Calma**, not blighted as yet by over-development. Here, a low cliff backing and a scattering of rocks and coves give the beach far more character than some of the seemingly endless stretches farther south.

The **Playa de Sotavento** is world-famous as a windsurfing center, with activity focused on the F2 school at the Sol Elite Gorriones Hotel. This has one of the best, and most isolated beach locations in all of the islands. Here the beach is very wide and flat, usually empty and, as the tides go out, also very wet. The dunes behind and a little farther to the south form an idyllic beach backdrop. *Urbanizaciones* spread relentlessly all the way down the coast to **Morro Jable**, which has some similarities with its northern sister Corralejo; both are ports and resorts, but in most other aspects are quite dissimilar. Whereas Corralejo is flat, rather dingy, without many hotels and restaurants of much class, and doesn't have much of its own beach, Morro Jable, built along the cliffs, is bright and airy, boasts numerous fine hotels and restaurants, and has miles of wonderful beaches. It is interesting to note that while Corralejo is a mainly British resort Morro Jable, on the other hand, is frequented predominantly by Germans. There are more fine beaches towards the southern tip of the island, but you will need a four-wheel-drive vehicle to get there. Jable, incidentally, is the name given to the huge quantities of sands of organic origins that are frequently blown to the surrounding beaches. Windsurfing, obviously, is all the rage around here, and numerous companies operate in and around Morro Jable and the other beaches of Jandía. The **Diving Center Félix** (3 Km {2 miles} north of Morro Jable) offers dives and equipment rental. Consider **Unisafari**; based in either Jandía or Corralejo, whose professional guides will take you on a seven-hour jeep safari to the most wild, least explored parts of the island.

WHAT TO DO

SPORTS

With the wonderfully mild climate of the Canaries, most sports are a year-round pleasure. Although water sports obviously dominate the scene there are some surprises — from Canaries wrestling to parachuting.

Fishing: Deep-sea fishing charters for the likes of shark, barracuda, marlin, and tuna are available at Los Cristianos Harbor (Tenerife), Puerto Rico (Gran Canaria), Peurto Calero (Lanzarote) and Corralejo (Fuerteventura).

Golf: The following are mostly 18-hole championship-standard golf courses:

On Tenerife, you'll find a multitude of courses including the Amarilla Golf and Country Club, Costa Golf Adeje, Golf Las Américas, Golf del Sur, and Centro de Golf Los Palos. Check with the various resorts for specific information. The Real Club de Golf de Las Palmas (situated on the rim of the Bandama volcanic crater, and the oldest in all Spain), and Campo de Golf (Maspalomas) are both on Gran Canaria. The Club de Golf de Costa Teguise is located in the north of Lanzarote.

Off Road Vehicle Adventures: These are becoming very popular, and a selection of them is listed below.

On Tenerife, *Quad Aventura* and *Tanarán Jeep Safari* are both located at Playa de las Américas or Puerto de La Cruz. *Miguel's Jeep-Safaris* operate on Gran Canaria.

Horseback-riding: There are stables with instructors at a number of locations, one of which is Los Caballos Horse Center. Take the La Caleta/Fañabe exit off N-822 and follow the signs to one of Tenerife's largest private plantations.

Mountain biking: Mountain bikes can be hired without any problems at most major resorts.

Two scuba-divers emerge from the water onto a Lanzarote beach.

Skydiving: Sky Dive, Gran Canaria, offer the really adventurous the chance to skydive. Don't worry, you will be attached to a qualified instructor who will control the dive. All you need is the nerve, and 27,000 ptas, €62.27.

Tennis: Most *urbanizaciones* and large hotels have their own courts. Public courts are few and far between.

Walking: All the islands except Fuerteventura and Lanzarote are good for serious walkers. Guided walks and special trails are mapped out for those intending to walk Mount Teide on Tenerife, and local tourist information offices may be able to help with trails in other national parks.

Water Sports

Scuba diving: This is becoming more and more popular, and the following companies offer excursions.

Diving Center Los Cristianos, <www.tenerifesub.home.ml.org>, (Tenerife). Canary Diving Adventures, Playa de Taurito; Atlantik Diving, Hotel Club de Mar, <www.clubde-mar.com/atlantic>, (Gran Canaria). Barrkuda Club, Playa Blanca, (Lanzarote) and Deep Blue, Caleta de Fuste, (Fuerteventura).

Surfing: A few beaches have the right conditions for surfing. Playa de Martiánez at Puerto de la Cruz (Tenerife) is very popular and you can also ride the waves at Playa de las Canteras, Las Palmas (Gran Canaria).

Swimming: There are many safe family beaches at all the major resorts, where breakwaters have created lagoon-like conditions. Be careful at all times on all other beaches. Even seemingly calm waters can hide dangerous undertows. Never swim alone. Some of the popular beaches have life-guards and many now use a flag system: red — don't swim; yellow — swim with caution; green — safe to swim.

Water-skiing: This is less popular than windsurfing in the Canaries, but is still usually available at all the major watersport resorts (see Scuba diving). Jet-skiing is also widely available.

Windsurfing: The Canaries are a windsurfers delight, particularly for the more experienced. Fuerteventura is the mecca. The winds at Sotavento Beach at Jandía are regularly strong, and in July the world championships are held here.

Spectator Sports

Canaries wrestling (*lucha canaria*): Rather like sumo wrestling, *lucha canaria* is a mixture of civilized ritual and caveman huffing and puffing. The basic aim is to throw the other man to the ground. The roots of the sport are hard to trace. Some say it came from Egypt, others that the Guanches may have devised it.

Fiestas and folklore exhibitions are still the tourist's best chance of seeing *la lucha*.

Vela Latina: *Lateens*, old-fashioned Canaries sailing rigs with triangular sails, race against each other on Saturday afternoons and Sunday mornings at Las Palmas and Puerto Rico on Gran Canaria, between April and September.

OTHER ACTIVITIES

Folklore

The folk music of the Canaries stands as a reminder that the archipelago has always been a bridge between Spain and the

New World. While most local songs sound Spanish, others would be perfectly at home in South America. Many can be traced far back into the islands' history.

Carnaval

For ten days each year, *Carnaval* is the time when thousands of Canarios celebrate the spring. Shops and businesses close, and young and old flood the streets in fancy dress, dancing to pulsating Latin rhythms.

Villages and groups of one kind or another dress according to chosen themes, with magnificent and often outrageous costumes that can take a whole year to put together. Bands

and dancers mingle with the elaborate floats. Tourists are treated with good-natured humor, and many don masks and costumes to join in the fun. The music and dancing continue until late, with parties everywhere.

Carnaval is biggest and best in Santa Cruz and Puerto de la Cruz on Tenerife and in Las Palmas on Gran Canaria, where it has all the razzmatazz of Rio's Carnaval and the Mardi Gras of New Orleans. Visitors come from all over the world for these

Clowns decorated with ice cream are completely appropriate at Carnaval.

events, and hotels are often full, so book well ahead if you plan to visit at this time of year.

Corpus Christi

After *Carnaval*, this is the most spectacular celebration on the islands, though it is of a completely different nature.

As an act of devotion at this religious time, colored volcanic sand, colored salt, or flower petals are painstakingly arranged on central paved areas to make up enormous artworks in the form of either elaborate abstract patterns or religious pictures, possibly copied from an Old Master. The most extravagant are to be seen in La Orotava and La Laguna on Tenerife, but Las Palmas on Gran Canaria and many other towns and villages throughout the islands also participate. The pictures are ruined, sometimes in a matter of moments, by the feet of the ensuing procession and certainly by the first rainfall. Only photographs preserve the memory of months of hard work.

Colorful fiestas of song and dance, food and wine, known as *Romerías*, follow hard on the heels of Corpus Christi to redress the sobriety.

FOR CHILDREN

With almost guaranteed sunshine, soft sandy beaches, and lots of amusement options off the beach, the more popular Canary Islands are perfect for children of all ages. Many hotels have special features for the young, ranging from poolside games to babysitters.

Ride a camel. Camel parks and rides are popular on the largest islands, where a dromedary (one hump, not two) will take you on a variety of trips. Two riders are accommodated at a time, slung on yoked seats on either side of the camel's neck, so it's a great adventure for two children. The most popular ones are at the Maspalomas sand dunes on Gran Canaria and the Montañas del Fuego on Lanzarote.

Go-carting. The carts never travel too quickly and are so low to the ground that they can't tip over. However, being so low they also give a thrilling sensation of speed, and your only problem will be getting your child off when it's time to go. Adult drivers are usually welcome too.

Karting Club Tenerife Arona (ten minutes from Playa de las Américas) has a normal speed track (admission: 1,300 ptas, [es]7.81), and a fast track (admission: 1,900 ptas, €11.42), and various other facilities. Open daily 10am–8pm. Gran Karting Club, Maspalomas (on Gran Canaria). An eight-minute drive will cost 1,500 ptas, €9.02 Gran Karting Club (2 km {about a mile} from the Lanzarote airport) has a senior track that is 1,281 m (1,400 yards) long with go-carts that can reach 80 Kph. (1,500 ptas, €9.02 for 8 minutes). There is also a junior track, 865 m (880 yards). Admission is 1,000 ptas, €6.01 for (ages 12–16), and 600 ptas, €3.61 (ages 5–11).

Go sailing. There are numerous trips throughout the islands on a variety of vessels and memorable whale and dolphin safaris for spotting pilot whales and friendly porpoises. However, do be aware that some of these trips can be too long for younger children.

Playa San Juan (between Playa de Américas and Los Gigantes) offers *Nostramo,* an original 1918 schooner; Playa de Américas/Los Cristianos has the only glass bottom catamaran in Puerto Colón: *Tropical Delfin.* In south Tenerife you can also try *Bonadea II* (Puerto Colón, dock pantalan 4); *Sea Quest* (Puerto Colón, dock pantalan 8).

Pick a banana. A trip to the banana plantation of Bananera El Guanche (see pages 26), outside Puerto de la Cruz, Tenerife, may not initially sound very exciting to a youngster. But the sight of whole banana fists growing wild is a novelty and the easy-to-follow video that precedes the self-guided tour makes learning fun. Adults get a banana liqueur at the end of the tour.

Watch the birdie (and the dolphins). There are several animal/bird parks in the islands, Tenerife's **Loro Park**, Gran Canaria's **Palmitos Park**, or Lanzarote's **Guinate Tropical Park** are all described in the Where To Go section of this guide. Others include the **Parque Las Aguilas**, Los Cristianos, Arona (Tenerife), which as the name implies, has an eagle show, all kinds of other birds and animals, and the new *JungleRaid* where kids of all ages can work their way through all kinds of obstacles.

Meet the Guanches. Older children are sure to be fascinated by the Guanche skulls, skeletons, and mummies kept at both the Museo Canario in Las Palmas and the Museo Arqueológico at Santa Cruz on Tenerife.

Submarine Trips: see Where To Go for info on these excursions. Puerto Colón, Playa de Américas (Tenerife); Peurto de Mogán (Gran Canaria); and Puerto Calero (Lanzarote).

SHOPPING

In 1852 the Canary Islands were declared a duty-free zone in order to stimulate the development of the archipelago and its ports as an Atlantic staging base. The plan worked, and the islands still boast some of the largest, busiest seaports in the whole of Spain.

In recent years the duty-free zone has been transformed into a trade-free zone, into which goods are imported without restrictions from all over the world, and the luxury tax is lower than in most countries.

Many shops in the main resorts stock cameras, calculators, watches, perfume, jewelry, leather goods, spirits, and tobacco — in fact, all the things that you can buy in airport duty-free

A souvenir shop in Santa Cruz de la Palma displays a variety of local knick-knacks.

shops. Aside from spirits and local tobacco, however, there are few real bargains.

Best Buys

Spirits and tobacco are the best bargains. Local brands of spirits are the cheapest, though rarely of high quality, and most international brands are also bargains. Local cigarettes are fairly rough but cigar smokers can find both price and quality. The cigars of La Palma in particular draw high praise.

For the really keen shopper, uncut gems, silver jewelry, silks, leatherwear, and furs may be of interest.

Indian Bazaars. Many of the shops selling luxury goods are owned by Indian entrepreneurs. Generally prices are flexible and haggling is accepted as part of the shopping process. You may assume that this is the case in any shop where prices are not marked.

Mercados. The most colorful shopping opportunities in the Canaries are at the open-air markets usually held on Sunday mornings. The Sunday morning *rastro* (flea market) near the port in Las Palmas is particularly good, and the Mercado de Nuestra Señora de Africa at Santa Cruz de Tenerife is recommended at any time.

Many provincial towns and villages hold Sunday markets where haggling is, of course, all part of the fun.

Island Products. The most celebrated local handicraft is embroidery. Many excursions visit craft workshops where local girls are engaged in delicate needlework on bedspreads, towels, and napkins and lace makers work on doilies, tablecloths, and other items. The beauty of these places is that you can see that what you are getting is authentic. Your purchase will also help keep the island's unique craft industry alive. Do not expect great bargains, however. If you are offered lace or embroidery cheap in the street it was probably made on a machine in the Far East.

Pottery is another possibility, albeit a more weighty one. There are several charmingly primitive styles practiced in the Canaries.

Centras artesanìas is a small chain of state-subsidized crafts shops on Tenerife selling pottery, wood carvings, jewelry, and paintings.

Last-Day Special. A few days before you are due to fly home, order some *strelitzias* — Bird of Paradise flowers. Compared with the price of exotic flora elsewhere these really are a bargain, even when packed into an air-freight box that makes them very easy to transport home.

NIGHTLIFE

In the main tourist centers of the Canaries you can find almost any style of nightlife you require, from extravagant and formal floorshows to cheap and rowdy karaoke bars.

Cabaret. Most of the large resorts, and some smaller ones, boast of an array of cabaret attractions. Some favorites include:

Mare Nostrum Resort (Playa de las Américas), <www.marenostrumresort.com>: Enjoy dinner, a show by The Platters, and entry to the casino (6,000 ptas, €36.06 per person); or dinner, a Flamenco show, half of The Platters' show and casino entry (8,400 ptas, €50.49 per person).

Gala Palace (San Eugenio): dinner at 8pm followed by a full cabaret show at 9:15pm (5,350 ptas, €32.15 per person).

Medieval Restaurant Show (Castillo San Miguel): dinner, drinks, a Medieval show and a concert by The Drifters — all in a mock castle (8pm–midnight, 5,350 ptas, €32.15 per person).

Puerto de La Cruz (Tenerife Palace): a meal at 8pm followed by a long-established cabaret show at 9:15pm (5,350 ptas, €32.15 per person).

Casino Palace Dinner Show (Casino Gran Canaria): always a spectacular cabaret with dinner 7:30 or 8pm and a show from 10pm–midnight. Prices range from 7,900 ptas, €47.48 for dinner with cava to 10,500 ptas, €63.11 for a gourmet meal with nice wines.

Gambling. Similar games are played in all of the casinos in the islands — French and American roulette, blackjack and craps. The minimum stake is from 200–500 ptas, €1.20-3.01 though slot machines cater to tighter budgets, and you will need your passport for security purposes. It is fascinating just watching the monied clientele in these places, not to mention the lightning reflexes of the croupiers, particularly as they scoop away the unfortunate bettors' gaming chips. The safest rule for amateurs is to decide in advance how much you can afford to lose (which you probably will) and stick rigidly to it.

Casino — Playa de las Américas, Hotel Gran Tenerife (open 8pm–4am; entrance 500 ptas, €3.01). Casino Royale — Mare Nostrum Resort, <www.marenostrumresort.com>, (admission with dinner shows only). Casino Taoro — Puerto de la Cruz is the most famous in betting circles (open 8pm to the early hours). Casino Las Palmas — Hotel Santa Catalina, Las Palmas de Gran Canaria (open daily 8pm–4am, until 5am on Friday and Saturday; admission 500 ptas, €3.01). Casino Gran Canaria — Hotel Meliá Tamarindos, Playa de San Agustín, Maspalomas (open daily 8pm–4am; admission 500 ptas, €3.01). Casino de Lanzarote — Puerto del Carmen (gambling machines open daily 11am–4am and gambling hall 8pm–4am.

Festivals

What with saints' days, religious and public holidays, village feast days, and two solid weeks of Carnaval, you would be very unlucky to visit the islands, particularly in the summer, and not catch some festivity or other. Here are a few of the most colorful events:

January: Cabalgata de los Reyes (Procession of the Three Kings): costumes, brass bands, camel cavalcades. Las Palmas (Gran Canaria); Santa Cruz, Garachico (Tenerife), Valle Gran Rey (Gomera).

February/March: Carnaval: winter opera and music festival (see below). Las Palmas (Gran Canaria); Santa Cruz (Tenerife).

Fiesta de Nuestra Señora de la Candelaria: La Oliva (Lanzarote).

Carnaval de Nuestra Señora del Rosario: festival of music and dance plus Canarian wrestling. Puerto del Rosario (Lanzarote).

March/April: Semana Santa (Holy Week): solemn pre-Easter processions in many towns and cities throughout the islands.

Commemoration of the Incorporation of the Islands under the Crown of Castille. Las Palmas (Gran Canaria).

May: spring festivals, opera. Santa Cruz (Tenerife).

Fiestas de la Cruz: processions, festivities, and fireworks. All places with Cruz (cross) in their name.

May/June: Fiestas de Corpus Christi: A religious festival celebrating the presence of the Body of Christ in the sacrament of the Eucharist (see below).

June: Romería de San Isidro: procession of ox-drawn carts laden with local produce. La Orotava (Tenerife).

July: Romería de San Benito: procession of ox-drawn carts laden with local produce. La Laguna (Tenerife).

Fiestas del Mar (Festival of the Sea): water sports, activities and religious ceremonies combined. Santa Cruz, Puerto de la Cruz (Tenerife).

Fiesta de San Buenaventura: important local festival featuring Canarian wrestling. Betancuria (Fuerteventura).

Fiesta de la Virgen del Carmen: a celebration of Our Lady of Carmen Virgin, the patron saint of all seamen. All islands, any village or town by the sea.

Romerías de Santiago Apóstol (Festival of St. James): pilgrimage, fireworks. Gáldar, San Bartolomé (Gran Canaria); Santa Cruz (Tenerife).

August: Fiesta de Nuestra Señora de las Nieves (Our Lady of the Snows): an interesting mixture of religious piety and general fun and games. Agaete (Gran Canaria); several locations (La Palma).

Fiesta de la Asunción (Assumption): re-enactment of the appearance of the Blessed Virgin to the Guanches. Candelaria (Tenerife).

Bajada de la Rama (Descent of the Branch): an ancient Guanche ceremony invoking rain. Agaete (Gran Canaria).

September: Semana Colón (Christopher Columbus Week): San Sebastián (Gomera).

Romería de la Virgen del Pino: religious festivities celebrating Our Lady of the Pine. Teror (Gran Canaria).

Fiestas del Santísimo Cristo: floats, flowers, and fireworks, processions, sports, classical theatre, and poetry readings. La Laguna, Tacaronte (Tenerife).

Fiesta de la Virgen de la Peña: island-wide celebrations of the patron saint of Fuerteventura. Pilgrimage to Vega del Rio de Palma, near Betancuria (Fuerteventura).

Fiesta de la Virgen de los Volcanes: a celebration of a miraculous deliverance from volcanic destruction. Mancha Blanca, Tinajo (Lanzarote).

October: Fiesta de Nuestra Señora de la Luz: flowers, fireworks and a maritime procession. Las Palmas (Gran Canaria).

November: Fiesta del Rancho de Animas: revival of ancient folklore. Teror (Gran Canaria).

December: Fiesta de Santa Lucía (The Festival of Lights): Máguez, near Haria (Lanzarote); Arucas, Gáldar, Santa Lucia (Gran Canaria).

EATING OUT

Travelers who treat local food and drink as an integral part of their holiday enjoyment will rarely be disappointed in the Canaries. There are some excellent Spanish restaurants in the islands, and cosmopolitan cuisine as elaborate or as downbeat as you please also thrives. You can choose to be served in candle-lit continental luxury or simply go to the nearest fast-food outlet.

If you want to sample real Canarian food look for the name *típico*, which indicates a good value, often country-style restaurant serving fresh local food.

Restaurants

Throughout Spain and the Canaries, restaurants are officially graded by a "fork" system. One fork is the lowest grade, five forks is the elite. However, these ratings are awarded according to the facilities and the degree of luxury that the restaurant offers, not the quality of the food. Five forks will therefore guarantee a hefty bill but not necessarily the finest food. Some of the best restaurants in the islands have fewer than five forks because their owners give priority to the quality of the food and wine rather than the standard of the furnishings.

A selection of recommended restaurants is enclosed at the end of this guide (see page 135). However, if in doubt, don't forget the universal criterion for sizing up a restaurant. Are the locals eating there?

All Spanish restaurants should offer a *menú del día* (daily special). This is normally three courses, including wine, at a very reasonable set price. If the waiter asks you "*¿Menú?*," he means, "Do you wish to order the *menú del día?*" If you want to read the menu, ask for "*La carta, por favor.*"

In all restaurants the prices on the menu include taxes and a service charge, but it is customary to leave a tip if you are served efficiently and cheerily. Five percent is acceptable, 10 percent is generous. Never eat in a restaurant that does not display prices. Also, remember to work out in advance how much your bill will be when ordering fish priced by the kilo.

Mealtimes are generally not as late in the Canaries as on the Spanish mainland. The peak hours are after 1pm for lunch and after 8pm for dinner, but you can get a meal in many places at just about any time of day.

Bars and Cafés

From sunrise to midnight, from the first coffee to the last brandy, the café is a very special institution in daily life in the Canaries. In practice there is little difference between a bar and a café, apart from the bias of the bar towards alcoholic drinks.

Most bars are noisy places, in keeping with the general decibel level in Spanish bars. The ubiquitous TV is almost always switched on, a radio or tape may well be playing simultaneously, and the gaming machine in the corner pumps out electronic staccato tones as the locals try to hit the jackpot.

Bars and cafés are the meeting places for both locals and tourists, to swap the day's news in pidgin English, Spanish, or German, or to shout at the TV screen whenever the football is on. The price of a cup of coffee buys you a ringside seat for as long as you care to stay; no one will rush you to leave or to buy another drink.

Wines and spirits are served at all hours everywhere in Spain, so don't raise an eyebrow when you see a local knocking back a large measure of colorless firewater first thing in the morning. You may also be surprised to see that children frequent bars with impunity. The Spanish consider this quite natural, even late at night.

Not exactly breakfast, lunch, or dinner — tapas are an all-day way to enjoy the local cuisine.

Bars and cafés usually include a service charge, but an additional small tip is the custom if you have spent any length of time in the establishment. Prices are 10-15 percent lower if you stand or sit at the bar rather than occupy a table.

Tapas

A *tapa* is a small portion of food served in a bar to encourage you to keep drinking instead of heading off to a restaurant for a meal. The word *tapa* means "lid" and comes from the custom of giving a free bite of food with a drink, the food served on a saucer atop the glass like a lid. Nowadays it is rare to see *tapas* given away, but *tapas* bars are more popular than ever.

Bonafide *tapas* bars, and indeed many simple bars, have a whole counter display of hot and cold snacks that make choosing very easy. Just point to the ones you like. Some of the most common Canarian (and Spanish) *tapas* are olives, meatballs, Russian salad, local cheese, wedges of Spanish omelette (*tor-*

tilla), *chorizo* (spicy salami-style sausage), *pulpo* (octopus) salad, *gambas* (prawns) with garlic dressing, mushrooms, deep fried crabmeat, and mountain-cured ham (*jamón serrano*).

Tapas are always accompanied by a basket of fresh bread. This is often lightly flavored with caraway and is delicious.

Portion control: *una tapa* is the smallest amount; *una ración* is half a small plateful and *una porción* is getting towards a meal in itself. Keep your enthusiasm to try everything on your first day in check. It is quite easy to spend more on *tapas* than on a good restaurant meal.

Breakfast

For Spaniards this is the least significant meal of the day. A coffee with a *tostado* (piece of toast) or a pastry is about the size of it. Down by the port you may well find the fishermen breakfasting on *calamares* (lightly battered squid), which is surprisingly delicious first thing in the morning. If you have a sweet tooth look for a place selling *churros*. These are deep-fried batter fritters, sugared and then traditionally dunked in coffee or hot chocolate.

Jamón Serrano

A leg of *jamón serrano* is a standard fixture in many Spanish restaurants and in nearly all *tapas* bars. The name means "mountain ham" and is often abbreviated simply to serrano. A tapa-sized portion comprises several wafer-thin slices on dry bread. The ham in use sits on a special holder horizontally behind the bar while others hang vertically from the ceiling. A small cup often hangs below to catch any juices. The hams are cured in the mountains of mainland Spain, the best coming from Huelva in Andalucía. You can gauge from the cost of a few thin slices that each leg represents a sizeable investment. When all the best meat has gone from the bone the leg is used for stewing or soup.

Most hotels offer huge breakfast buffets, including a truly international array of cereals, juices, dried and fresh fruits, cold meats and cheeses, plus bacon and eggs. Many cafés also cater to tourists by offering a *desayuno completo* of orange juice, bacon, eggs, toast, and coffee. Of course, in the English resorts it is not at all difficult to find a full English breakfast–arguably England's finest contribution to cuisine, at almost any hour of the day.

Canaries Cuisine

The local cooking is usually wholesome, filling, and delicious. Unfortunately for those in search of the real thing it is often much easier to find a "real British pub" than a *típico*. When you do, look for the following:

Rancho canario — a rich meat and vegetable soup thickened with *gofio*, the Canarian staff of life. *Gofio* was first eaten by the prehistoric Guanches. It used to be made of crushed barley or rye but now it is usually wholemeal or maize meal, toasted and milled.

Garbanzo compuesto — chick-pea stew with potatoes, also made with *gofio*.

Puchero — a stew of meat and vegetables.

Potaje — a rich, thick vegetable soup.

All of the above are served as starters but for those with lesser appetites are meals in themselves.

Mojo picón — a red piquant sauce composed mainly of paprika and chili. It is often spicy, so approach cautiously.

Mojo verde — by contrast, a cool green herb sauce usually made of coriander and parsley. An excellent side to grilled fish.

Papas viudas (literally "widow potatoes") — roast potatoes with carrots, peas, parsley, olives, green pepper, ham, and onions.

Sancocho — a stew of salted fish (usually sea bass or salt cod) with sweet potatoes, vegetables, and *mojo picón*.

Conejo en salmorejo — rabbit in a spicy sauce made with *mojo picón*.

Papas arrugadas (literally wrinkled potatoes) — potatoes baked in their skins in very salty water, rolled in rock salt, and generally served with *mojo picón*.

Surrounded by the Atlantic Ocean, the Canarians naturally consider fish a vital part of their diet. You will find most kinds of seafood here, from octopus to swordfish and local varieties such as *vieja* ("widow" fish) and *cherna* (a type of grouper). Don't underestimate the humble sardine; they are delicious straight off the barbecue or grill (*a la parilla*).

Meat is just as common on most menus, even though much of it is imported from mainland Spain or South America. Prices are very reasonable and the quality is usually good.

Goat's-milk cheeses vary from island to island and are certainly worth trying. You will also see *Manchego*, a famous hard, unpasteurized cheese from the mainland.

Canarians do not go in for desserts much, but do look for *bien me sabe* ("How good it tastes"), a confection of honey, almonds, and rum. Cakes and pastries are best sampled in a *dulcería*, a cross between a tea-room and an ordinary café. El

---

Burial of the Sardine

Of all the island festivities, Burial of the Sardine (held during *Carnaval*) is surely the most bizarre. A huge board and timber sardine of *Jaws* proportions is hauled solemnly on a large float from an appointed place to the sea. Accompanying it are hundreds of "mourners" making the most incredible din with their mock anguish, weeping and wailing in the wake of the "deceased" fish. Beauty queens, transvestites-for-the-night, and whole families dressed in stylized black mourning gear make up a completely surreal funeral party. At the sea the sardine is ritually burned and a great fireworks display is given.

Almonds, figs, and apricots tipify indigenous Canarian cuisine — equally tasty and wholesome treats.

Hierro is noted for its *quesadilla*, a fluffy cake made with lemon and cheese, though quite unlike a conventional cheesecake.

Spanish Cuisine

Since the Canaries are Spanish and a good number of tourists are from Spain, there are some excellent Spanish restaurants on the islands. Look for these specialties:

Gazpacho — a chilled soup made from tomatoes, peppers, cucumbers and garlic, served with various crudités.

Sopa de ajo — a thick soup of chopped garlic, with paprika, breadcrumbs, and eggs.

Huevos a la flamenca — baked eggs, asparagus, red pepper, and peas atop a sausage-and-ham base.

Paella — Spain's most famous dish is named after the large, black iron pan in which it is cooked. Ingredients vary, but it is basically rice cooked in stock, flavored and colored with saffron, plus a mixture of chicken or rabbit, fish, shellfish, sausage, pork, and peppers. By tradition, this is a Spanish lunchtime meal; however, it is usually on offer as an evening meal in many restaurants catering to tourists.

Alcoholic Drinks

In Elizabethan times, Canaries wine was served at all the top tables in Europe. Tastes may have changed, but the local wines are still very good. Unfair as it may seem, local wines are dearer than table wines imported from the mainland because they are made on a much smaller scale.

Several of the vines flourish because of the volcanic soil, giving the wine a rich, full flavor. Historically, Canaries wines were of the Malmsey (*malvasía*) variety. These tend to be very sweet, but there are drier varieties that retain the same rich, distinctive bouquet. You are more likely to be offered local wines in country restaurants than in the big resorts.

Rum (*ron*) may conjure up visions of the Caribbean, but it

is also made in the Canaries and is very popular here. It is often mixed with cola in a *Cuba libre*. A liqueur called *ronmiel* (literally rum honey) is a specialty of La Gomera. Local distilleries also produce fruit-based liqueurs; particularly banana, but also orange and other tropical flavors. *Sangría* is probably the most popular tourist drink throughout Spain. It is a mixture of red wine, orange and lemon juices, brandy, and mineral

The open doorway of a bar in Teguise beckons to those passing by.

water topped with lots of sliced fruit and ice. This perfect hot-weather concoction can pack quite a punch.

Sherry *(Jerez)*, that most famous of Spanish drinks, is not as popular in the Canaries as it is on the mainland, but together with Spanish brandy (colloquially known as *coñac*), Spanish-style champagne *(cava)*, and a whole host of international brand names, it is available in all good bars and served in huge devil-may-care measures.

> In Shakespeares's days *sherry wine* was called *sack* or *sherries sack*. Sack derived from the Spanish word "*sacar*" (to export), while sherries comes from the name of the town *Jerez*, where this wine originated.

Supermarket shelves are full of the same names at eye-popping prices and are always much cheaper than airport duty-free shops.

Canarian beer *(cerveza)* is usually Tropical or Dorada lager. The latter is recommended. Beer is served either draft or in bottles measuring one-third of a liter. Draft measures vary but basically if you want a small beer ask for "*una cerveza pequeña.*"

"*Una cerveza grande*" can vary in size, but is often around the size of a US pint. Remember that Spanish lager is a little stronger than most US beers.

Tea, Coffee, and Soft Drinks

The Spanish usually drink coffee *(café)* rather than tea *(té)*. This can be either *solo* (small and black), *con leche* (a large cup made with milk, often in a frothy cappuccino-style), or *cortado* (a small cup with a little milk). It is strong and very tasty. Mineral water *(agua mineral)* is either sparkling *(agua con gas)* or still *(agua sin gas)*. Ice-cream parlors sell *granizado*, slushy iced fruit juice in several flavors, and freshly pressed orange juice *(zumo de naranjas)*, the latter being surprisingly expensive.

HANDY TRAVEL TIPS

An A–Z Summary of Practical Information

A

ACCOMMODATION

Most accommodation in the Canaries is designed for family package vacations and tends to be of a medium-high international standard. Aside from hotels there are apartments and "aparthotels," where each room has its own kitchen facilities yet retains all the trappings of a hotel. Package vacations tend to provide accommodation in hotel complexes and self-catering apartments, while those traveling independently will find a wide range of options. If you plan to visit during the high season (late Nov–Mar), book accommodation well in advance through a travel agent or directly with the hotel. For a comprehensive listing of accommodations and rates throughout Spain, consult the Guía Oficial de Hoteles — available from The Spanish National Tourist Office (see TOURIST INFORMATION OFFICES on page 123).

By law, prices must be displayed in the reception and in the rooms. Meals (including breakfast) are not usually included in the basic rate, and a sales tax of 4.5% IGIC.

Establishments are graded by each of the 17 autonomous governments by a system that allows for many categories of accommodation and variations in each category. A hotel may be rated from one-star to 5-stars, and 5-star Gran Lujo (GL) that signifies top-of-the-range quality. However, it's not easy to find cheap accommodation in the major resorts, with the majority of places being at least 3- or 4-star hotels. The really large towns, such as Santa Cruz de Tenerife and Las Palmas de Gran Canaria, will have a selection of lower-rated places.

Paradors are state-run hotels, often housed in castles or other historic buildings, which are of special interest to motorists, as they are often located outside of towns and in rural areas. Advance booking is highly recommended. For information and bookings in the USA and Canada contact Marketing Ahead, 433 Fifth Avenue, New York, NY; Tel. 800- 223-1356 or (212)686-9213; fax (212)686-0271; e-mail mahrep@aol.com. In Spain contact the Paradores de Turismo,

Canary Islands

Central de Reservas, Requena, 3, 28013 Madrid; Tel. (91)5166666; fax (91) 5166657; <www.parador.es>. In the U.K., Tel. (171)402-8181; fax (171)724-9503.

a single/double room	**una habitación sencilla/doble**
with bath/shower	**con baño/ducha**
What's the rate per night?	**Cuál es el precio por noche?**

AIRPORTS *(aeropuertos)*
All the islands have commercial airports.

Province of Santa Cruz de Tenerife (telephone code 922):
Tenerife: Tenerife-Sur Reina Sofia: Tel. 75 92 00; Tenerife-Norte Los Rodeos: Tel. 63 56 35; La Palma: Tel. 42 61 00; El Hierro: Tel. 55 08 78 and La Gomera: Tel. 87 30 00.

Province of Las Palmas de Gran Canaria (telephone code 928):
Las Palmas de Gran Canaria: Tel. 57 90 00; Lanzarote: Tel. 86 05 00 and Fuerteventura: Tel. 81 14 50.

Every airport is served by taxis and car-hire companies, and the major airports also have regular bus services.

 B

BUDGETING FOR YOUR TRIP
To give you an idea of what to expect, here's a list of some average prices in pesetas. They can only be approximate, as prices vary from place to place, and inflation in Spain, as elsewhere, creeps up relentlessly. Consider US \$1 equal to about 150 ptas, €0.90 — the lowest you are likely to get. However, it can range upwards by ten or more pesetas to the dollar.

Accommodation: Rates for a double room can range from as low as 4,000– 5,000 ptas, €24.04-30.05 at a *pensión* or *hostal* to as much as 60,000 to 70,000 ptas, €360.61-420.71 at a top-of-the-range 5-star hotel. A nice 4-star hotel will cost in the range of 15,000–20,000 ptas,

€90.15-120.20. Beware — rates increase during the high season, beginning around late November and culminating with the *Carnaval*.

Apartments: Prices vary widely, but here are averages per night for a family apartment: 4 keys — 12,000 ptas, €72.12 and above; 3 keys — 6,800–12,000 ptas, €40.87-72.12; 2 keys — 4,500–6,800 ptas, 27.05-40.87; 1 key — under 4,500 ptas, €27.05. Discounts are often available for bookings of a week or more.

Attractions: Tenerife: *Bananera El Guanche* 675 ptas, €4.06, *Loro Parque* 1,950 ptas, €11.72. Gran Canaria: *Palmitos Parque* 1,900 ptas, €11.42. Lanzarote: *Montañas del Fuego* 1,000 ptas, €6.01, *Jameos del Agua* 1,000 ptas, €6.01. General: Submarine trips about 3,900 ptas, €23.44; water parks around 1,500 ptas, €9.02.

Car rental: Prices vary: if you rent before your trip starts; if you rent from a local company or one in your own country; how long you want the car; if you want an automatic or manual transmission; what insurance coverage you want, or are obliged, to purchase.

Entertainment: Cinema from 600 ptas, €3.61; nightclub (entry and first drink) from 3,000 ptas, €18.03; discotheque from 1,000 ptas, €6.01. Amusement park (per day) 4,000 ptas, €24.04/adult or 3,000 ptas, €18.03/child.

Meals and drinks: These vary considerably. In a bar a Continental breakfast (fresh orange juice and toast), will cost around 500 ptas. The cheapest three-course meal, *menú del día* with one drink, in a small bar/restaurant, will be around 800–900 ptas, €4.81-5.41. Dinner in a medium level restaurant will be about 3,000 ptas, €18.03 per person, including wine. At the top restaurants expect to pay at least 6,000 to 7,000 ptas, €36.06-42.07 per person, plus wine.

In a bar a beer, small bottle or glass, will range from 100–150 ptas, €0.60-0.90; coffee 100–150 ptas, €0.60-0.90; Spanish brandy

250–300 ptas, €1.50-1.80; soft drinks from 150 ptas, €0.90; and a glass of local wine about 50 ptas, €0.30.

Shopping: By far the cheapest places are the very large hypermarkets where, for example, a can of *San Miguel* beer might cost around 65 ptas, €0.39. In a small corner store or *Supermercado* (supermarket) that same beer might cost between 100–125 ptas, €0.60-0.75, and similar price differentials exist for most other goods.

Sports: Golf green fees (per day) range from around 7,500–9,000 ptas, €45.08-54.09. Tennis court fees start at around 1,000 ptas, €6.01/hour. Horse back riding starts at about 2,000 ptas, €12.02/hour.

I want to change some pounds/dollars.	**Quiero cambiar libras/dólares.**
Do you accept traveler's checks?	**¿Acepta usted cheques de viajero?**
Can I pay with this credit card?	**¿Puedo pagar con esta tarjeta de crédito?**

C

CAR HIRE *(coches de alquiler)* (See also DRIVING.)
Normally you must be over 21 to rent a car, and you will need a valid driver's license that you have held for at least 12 months, your passport and a major credit card — cash deposits are prohibitively large.

If renting before you go, **Auto-europe**, Tel. 800-223-5555, is the best and largest organization in North America. However, the Canary Islands present two difficulties: The names of the islands and principal towns can be very similar to those not familiar with them (like most people in North America). This can cause problems in the lesser known islands. Second, those that can only drive automatic cars may have problems with Auto-europe, as the companies they deal with have few such cars available anywhere, let alone off the main islands.

There are actually numerous local companies, but generally these are indeed local to each island and again, automatic cars will be a major problem. There is one company, however, **CICAR (Canary Islands Car)**, Tel. (928)82 29 00; <www.cicar.com>, that has been in business for over thirty years and is the only one to have offices on each island and a ready availability of automatic cars. Also, 90% of the cars have airbags, 80% power steering and 95% protected sides, and the price includes 100% insurance cover. Their offices are easily recognizable by the modern, colorful, logo designed by no less than César Manrique.

I'd like to rent a car.	**Quisiera alquilar un coche.**
for one day/week.	**por un día/una semana.**
Please include full insurance.	**Haga el favor de incluir el seguro a todo riesgo.**

CLIMATE

Despite the popular concept that sunshine is guaranteed here, it is impossible to generalize about the islands. It may be pouring with chilly rain on La Gomera or La Palma, while sunbathers bake on Fuerteventura. The mountainous nature of Gran Canaria and the north/south divide of Tenerife means that the weather can be completely different at opposite ends of each island.

There are two rules of thumb: The easterly islands are drier and warmer than the westerly ones (Lanzarote and Fuerteventura are normally a little warmer than Gran Canaria); the sunnier, warmer weather is likely to be found on the south side of an island.

Be prepared for winds: In spring there is a cold and wet gust from the northwest, and in autumn the famous sirocco.

Approximate monthly average temperature:

	J	F	M	A	M	J	J	A	S	O	N	D
°C	17	16	17	18	21	22	23	24	23	22	20	18
°F	64	62	64	64	68	71	74	75	74	70	69	64

CLOTHING

In addition to summer clothes and beachwear, don't forget a sweater or jacket for evenings. For excursions to high altitudes you will also need warmer clothing and some sturdy shoes. During the winter some protection from the rain may well come in handy.

Casual wear is the norm, though in five-star hotels, the best restaurants, and the casino, a jacket and tie (though not obligatory) will not be out of place for men.

Topless bathing has become quite common, and is acceptable at most hotel pools. Shorts and mini-skirts should not be worn when visiting religious places.

COMPLAINTS

By law, all hotels and restaurants must have official complaint forms *(hoja de reclamaciones)* and produce them on demand. The original of this triplicate document should be sent to the Ministry of Tourism; one copy remains with the establishment involved and one copy is given to you. Try to resolve your problem before going through this procedure, as it will be difficult for you to succeed in any claims once you are off the island. However, the very action of asking for the *hoja* may resolve the problem in itself, as tourism authorities take a serious view of malpractice, and can revoke or suspend licenses.

You should also inform the local tourist office, or in serious cases the local police, of any complaints and seek their assistance.

CUSTOMS *(aduana)* **AND ENTRY FORMALITIES**

Most visitors, including citizens of all EU countries (including the UK), the USA, Canada, Ireland, Australia, and New Zealand, require only a valid passport to enter Spain. British tourists may no longer enter Spain on a visitor's passport. Visitors from South Africa must have a visa; contact the Spanish Consulate General, 37 Short Market St., Cape Town, 8001; Tel. (27) 21 422 2415; fax (27) 21 422-2328. The web site <www.raipttp.co.za/cargo/visa/cana-cpt.html> also gives full details of the requirements for these visas.

Currency restrictions. Tourists may bring an unlimited amount of Spanish or foreign currency into the country. On departure you must declare any amount beyond the equivalent of 1,000,000 pesetas.

Since the Canaries are a free-trade zone, there is no restriction on what you may bring in with you as a tourist. However, it would be absurd to buy duty-free cigarettes or spirits at your airport of departure as you will find the same items much cheaper on the islands.

CRIME

The most common crime against the tourist in the Canaries (as in all of Spain) is theft from rental cars. If you park overnight in the street in one of the big towns or resorts, as you may have to, there is every chance that your car will be broken into. Never leave anything of value in your car. Use the safe deposit box in your room for all valuables, including your passport. Burglaries of vacation apartments do occur, so keep doors and windows locked when you are absent and while you are asleep. You must report all thefts to the local police within 24 hours for your own insurance purposes, but do not hold out any hope of getting your property back.

I want to report a theft.   **Quiero denunciar un robo.**

DRIVING

Driving conditions. The rules are the same as in mainland Spain and the rest of the Continent: drive on the right, pass on the left, yield right of way to all vehicles coming from your right. Speed limits are 120 km/h (74 mph) on motorways, 100 km/h (62 mph) on dual highways, and 50 km/h (31 mph) in built-up areas.

Roads vary from six-lane highway (in Santa Cruz de Tenerife) to primitive tracks (any rural area). In every main city, and even in smaller provincial ones, traffic is appalling and one-way systems confusing. Do not drive unless you have to in these towns.

Canary Islands

Many roads are narrow and twisting, though quite delightful as long as you are not in a hurry. The locals often are, so move over and let them pass, if you can. Always slow down when passing through villages. Be aware that at any time you may suddenly come across a herd of goats, a donkey and cart, a large pothole, or rocks falling around the next bend.

Always allow more time than you think a journey will take from simply looking at the map. Driving on mountain roads all day can be very tiring, so take frequent breaks.

Gasoline. Unleaded gasoline is known as *sin plomo*.

Parking. Parking in all the capitals, and the other larger towns is at the least very difficult, and often verges on the near impossible. It is an offense to park the car facing against the traffic, and if your hotel is in a pedestrianized area you may have to park a long way away.

Traffic police. Armed civil guards (Guardia Civil) patrol the roads on black motorcycles. In towns the municipal police handle traffic control. If you are fined for a traffic offense, you will have to pay on the spot.

Rules and regulations. Always carry your driving license with you. It is also a good idea to have a photocopy of the important pages of your passport with you.

Seat belts are compulsory everywhere. Children under the age of ten must travel in the rear.

Road signs. Aside from the standard pictographs you may encounter the following:

Aparcamiento	Parking
Desviación	Detour
Obras	Road works
Peatones	Pedestrians
Peligro	Danger
Salida de camiones	Truck exit

¿Se puede aparcar aquí?	Can I park here?
Llénelo, por favor, con super.	Fill the tank please, top grade.
Ha habido un accidente.	There has been an accident.

Fluid measures

Distance

E

ELECTRICITY *(corriente eléctrica)*

220V/50Hz AC is now standard, but older installations of 125 volts can still be found. Check! An adapter for Continental-style two-pin sockets will be needed; American 110V appliances will also require a transformer.

EMBASSIES AND CONSULATES *(consulado)*

Province of Santa Cruz de Tenerife:
Tenerife (telephone code 922):

Santa Cruz de Tenerife: United Kingdom: Plaza Weyler, 8, 1st Floor; Tel. 28 68 63; fax 28 99 03; open Monday–Friday 8am–2pm. Republic of Eire: Calle Castillo, 8, Fourth Floor A, 38002; Tel. 24 56 71; fax 24 99 57; open Monday–Friday 9am–1pm.

Province of Las Palmas de Gran Canaria:
Gran Canaria (telephone code 928):

Las Palmas de Gran Canaria: United States of America: Calle Franchy Roca, 5, 35007; Tel. 27 12 59/22 25 52; fax 22 58 63; open Monday–Friday 10am–1pm. United Kingdom: Edificio Cataluña,

Canary Islands

Calle de Luis Morote, 6, Third Floor, 35007; Tel. 26 25 08/26 25 12; fax 26 77 74; e-mail islands@pasanet.es; open Monday–Friday 8:30am–1:30pm. South Africa: Calle Franchy Roca, 5, 6th Floor; Tel. 22 60 04; fax 22 60 15; open Monday–Friday 10am–midday.

Most European countries have consular offices in Santa Cruz and/or Las Palmas.

If you run into trouble with the authorities or the police, contact your consulate for advice.

Where is the American/British consulate?	**¿Dónde está el consulado americano/británico?**

EMERGENCIES *(urgencia)*

112 is the emergency number throughout the Canary Islands.

GETTING THERE

By air. See also AIRPORTS. At the time of writing there were no direct flights to the Canary Islands from the USA, although some charter flights do go directly, and that necessitates a change of planes either in Madrid or Casablanca.

IBERIA, Tel. 1 800 772-4642; <www.iberia.com>; has flights from New York City and Miami to Madrid, and connections to all the islands. **air europa**, Tel. (718) 244-7055; fax (718) 656 04 08; <www.air-europa.com>; has flights from New York City to Madrid, and connections from there to Tenerife North and South, and Lanzarote. An interesting alternative, and one that allows for a stopover in North Africa, is to use **Royal Air Maroc**, Tel. 800-344-6726, <www.kingdomofmorocco.com>, service between New York City and Casablanca, and their connection on to Las Palmas, Gran Canaria. For those preferring to avoid New York City and JFK, **Spanair**, Tel. 1 888 545 5757, <www.spanair.com>, has services from Dulles Airport, Washington DC, to Madrid, with connections from there to Tenerife, Gran Canaria, Lanzarote and Fuerteventura.

By ship. Trasmediterranea, Tel. 902 45 46 45; <www.trasmediter-ranea.es>; has a limited number of sailings from Cádiz, Tel. (956)22 20 38, on the Spanish mainland to Santa Cruz Tenerife, Tel. (922)28 61 06, Las Palmas de Gran Canaria, Tel. (928)47 41 11 and Santa Cruz de La Palma, Tel. (922)41 39 53.

GAY AND LESBIAN TRAVELERS

Major resorts in the Canary Islands have developed facilities for gay and lesbian travelers, including dedicated hotels. The Playa del Ingles has The Yumbo Center; a shopping center by day and a pre-dominantly "gay center" by night with bars, restaurants and clubs.

GUIDES AND TOURS

All the major islands are comprehensively covered by tour operators, whose coaches take tourists to anywhere and everywhere that is worth seeing, both day and night.

HEALTH & MEDICAL CARE

Anything other than basic emergency treatment can be very expen-sive, and you should not leave home without adequate insurance, preferably including coverage for an emergency flight home in the event of serious injury or illness.

British and Irish citizens are entitled to free emergency hospital treat-ment — you should obtain form E111 from a post office before you leave in order to qualify. You may have to pay part of the price of treatment or medicines; keep receipts so that you can claim a refund back home.

Farmacias (chemist/drugstore) are usually open during normal shopping hours. After hours, at least one per town remains open all night, called *farmacia de guardia,* and its location is posted in the window of all other *farmacias* and in the local newspapers.

Where's the nearest (all-night) chemist?	**¿Dónde está la farmacia (de guardia) más cercana?**

Canary Islands

I need a doctor/dentist.	**Necesito un médico/dentista.**	
sunburn/sunstroke	**quemadura del sol/una insolación**	
an upset stomach	**molestias de estómago**	

HOLIDAYS *(día de fiesta)*

In addition to these Spanish national holidays, many purely local and lesser religious, civic, and other holidays are celebrated in various towns of the archipelago (see Festivals, pages 91).

1 January	**Año Nuevo**	New Year's Day
6 January	**Epifanîa**	Epiphany
19 March	**San José**	St Joseph's Day
1 May	**Día del Trabajo**	Labor Day
25 July	**Santiago Apóstol**	St James's Day
15 August	**Asunción**	Assumption
12 October	**Día de la Hispanidad**	Discovery of America Day (Columbus Day)
1 November	**Todos los Santos**	All Saints' Day
25 December	**Navidad**	Christmas Day

Movable dates:

Jueves Santo	Maundy Thursday
Viernes Santo	Good Friday
Lunes de Pascua	Easter Monday (Catalonia only)
Corpus Christi	Corpus Christi
Inmaculada Concepción	Immaculate Conception (normally 8 December)

LANGUAGE

The Spanish spoken in the Canary Islands is slightly different from that of the mainland. For instance, islanders don't lisp when they pronounce the letters c or z. The language of the Canaries is spoken with a slight lilt, reminiscent of the Caribbean: A number of New World words and expressions are used. The most commonly heard are *guagua* (pronounced wah-wah), meaning bus, and *papa* (potato). In tourist areas German, English, and some French is spoken, or at least understood.

The *Berlitz Spanish Phrasebook and Dictionary* covers most situations you may encounter in your travels in Spain and the Canaries.

Do you speak English?	**¿Habla usted inglés?**
I don't speak Spanish.	**No hablo español.**

LOST PROPERTY *(Objetos perdidos)*

The first thing to do when you discover you have lost something is obviously to retrace your steps. If you still cannot find the missing item, report the loss to the Municipal Police or the Guardia Civil (see POLICE). Lost property offices throughout the islands are as follows.

Province of Santa Cruz de Tenerife: Tenerife:
Airport North, Los Rodeos; Tel. 63 58 55. Airport South Reina Sofía; Tel. 75 93 91. Santa Cruz de Tenerife; Tel. 60 60 92. Costa Adeje; Tel. 71 06 06/79 31 21. Garachico; Tel. 83 00 00.

I've lost my wallet/ pocketbook/passport.	**He perdido mi cartera/bolso/ pasaporte.**

MEDIA

Radio and television *(radio; televisión.)* Most hotels have satellite TV with several stations in many languages. The larger islands all include some English language news and tourist information in their programming. Local radio stations broadcasting in English include WAVES FM 96.8, the only station that can be heard on all seven islands, although not in all parts.

Newspapers and magazines. Major British and Continental newspapers are on sale in the Canaries the day after publication. English-language publications with Canarian news and tourist information include:

Province of Santa Cruz de Tenerife: Tenerife: *Here & Now*, a bi-weekly newspaper available free in hotels; *La Gaceta,* a free weekly newspaper in Spanish, English and German; *The Western Sun,* issued free and *The Paper,* published bi-weekly and also free.

Province of Las Palmas de Gran Canaria: Gran Canaria: *Mogán News*, in English and German (free); **Lanzarote:** *Gazette News* and *Lanzarote Is It* (both free monthlies); **Fuerteventura:** *Fuerteventura Grapevine (free; monthly)*, <http://personal1.iddeo.es/gdgvine/fuertegvine.html>.

Throughout the Islands: The free *Holiday Gazette & Tourist Guide* available monthly the *Island Sun*, <www.island-sun-newspaper.com>, published bi-weekly and available at newsagents for 150 pesetas, and *Island Connections*, <www.ic-web.com>, free.

MONEY MATTERS

Currency. The monetary unit throughout Spain is the peseta (abbreviated pta/ptas).

Coins: 1, 5, 10, 25, 50, 100, 200, and 500 pesetas. Besides the fact that they increase in size according to value and with the 25 ptas coin having a hollow center, they alternate in color according to their value with (1 pta. being silver and the 5 ptas gold etc). In 2000 a new, commemorative, 2,000 ptas coin will be issued.

Banknotes: 1,000 (green), 2,000 (orange), 5,000 (brown), and 10,000 (blue) pesetas.

The *Euro* remains an electronic/banking currency until 1 January 2002, when it will be introduced in the form of bills and coins. After a six-month transition period, on 1 July 2002, the Euro will become Spain's single currency.

Banking hours are usually from 9am–2pm Monday–Friday, but watch out for all the holidays for which Spain is famous!

Many travel agencies and other businesses displaying a *cambio* sign will change foreign currency into pesetas. All larger hotels will also change guests' money, but the rate is slightly less than at the bank. Traveler's checks always get a better rate than cash. Take your passport with you when changing money or traveler's checks.

Credit cards, traveler's checks, Eurocheques. These are accepted in most hotels, restaurants, and big shops.

Where's the nearest bank/ currency exchange office?	**¿Dónde está el banco más cercano/la oficina de cambio más cercana?**
I want to change some dollars/pounds.	**Quiero cambiar dólares/ Libres esterlina.**
Do you accept traveler's checks?	**¿Acepta usted cheques de viajero?**
Can I pay with this credit card?	**¿Puedo pagar con esta tarjeta de crédito?**

OPENING HOURS

Shops and offices and other businesses generally observe the afternoon siesta, opening 9:30am/10am–1:30pm/2pm and 4:30pm/5pm– 7:30pm/8pm, but in tourist areas many places now stay open all day.

P

POLICE *(policía)*

There are three police forces in Spain. The best known is the *Guardia Civil* (Civil Guard). Each town also has its own *Policía Municipal* (municipal police), whose uniform varies depending on the town and season but is mostly blue and gray. The third force, the *Cuerpo Nacional de Policía,* a national anti-crime unit, can be recognized by its light brown uniform. All police officers are armed. Spanish police are strict but courteous to foreign visitors.

Where is the nearest police station?	**¿Dónde está la comisaría más cercana?**

POST OFFICES *(correos)*

These are for mail and telegrams, not telephone calls. Stamps *(sellos or timbres)* are sold at any tobacconist's *(tabacos)* and by most shops selling postcards. See the web site, <www.correos.es>.

Mailboxes are painted yellow. If one of the slots is marked *extranjero,* it is for letters abroad.

Where is the (nearest) post office?	**¿Dónde está la oficina de correos (más cercana)?**
A stamp for this letter/postcard, please.	**Por favor, un sello para esta carta/tarjeta.**

PUBLIC TRANSPORTATION

Airlines. A number of airlines operate flights between the islands. **Binter Canarias**, Tel. 902 40 05 00, a recently privatized subsidiary of IBERIA, has the most; **air europa** Tel. 902 40 15 01; **Spanair** Tel. 902 13 14 15; **NAYSA** Tel. 900 71 77 27; and **Atlantic Airways** Tel. (928)26 16 83, reservations (928)78 65 31.

Bus services. Within the large towns buses run often and are fast and cheap, with tickets purchased on board and change given. Bus services around the islands vary in frequency and scope.

Province of Santa Cruz de Tenerife:
(telephone code 922):

On Tenerife: Buses (guagas), operated by *Transportes Interurbanos de Tenerife, SA* (TITSA); Tel. 53 13 00 — 24-hours a day in Spanish or English;<www.titsa.com>. The buses are easily identifiable by their green color and run to almost every part of the island with surprising frequency.

On La Gomera: Buses are operated by *Servicio Regular La Gomera*, Tel. 87 14 18 and there are just three routes.

On La Palma: Buses are operated by *Transportes Insular*, Tel. 41 19 24. Only a few routes will be of real interest to visitors: Santa Cruz de La Palma-Los Cancajos-Aeropuerto and back; and Santa Cruz de La Palma-Los Llanos de Aridane. This line runs from coast to coast and passes the *Centro de Visitantes* (Visitors Center) of the Caldera de Taburiente National Park.

Province of Las Palmas de Gran Canaria:
(telephone code 928):

On Gran Canaria: Besides the city bus services, two companies operate long distance routes. **SALCAI**; Tel. 38 11 00; <www.salcai.es>; operate services down the east coast, throughout the south of the island and up to Cruz de Tejeda. **UTINSA**; Tel. 36 83 35; operates services in the northern third of the island, with the most interesting route for visitors being **Line 305** between Las Palmas and Tejeda.

On Lanzarote: The three lines of most interest to visitors are: **Line 1** between Arrecife and Costa Teguise; **Line 2** between Arrecife and Puerto del Carmen; and **Line 3** between Arrecife and Playa Blanca.

On Fuerteventura: Buses are operated by *Tiadhe*, who have services between the most important towns. Note: For all north/south trips you must change in Puerto del Rosario.

Ferry services. There are numerous ferry services between the islands (and even the Spanish mainland) operated by *Líneas Fred*

Canary Islands

Olsen, <www.fredolsen.es>; *Trasmediterranea*, <www.trasmediter-ranea.es>; *Naviera Armas* Tel. (928)22 72 82; and *Trasarmas*.

Between Lanzarote and Fuerteventura: Líneas Fred Olsen and Naviera Armas (between Playa Blanca, Lanzarote and Corralejo, Fuerteventura); Trasmediterranea (between Arrecife, Laznarote and Puerto del Rosario, Fuerteventura).

Between Lanzarote and Gran Canaria: Naviera Armas (between Arrecife, Lanzarote and Las Palmas de Gran Canaria).

Between Lanzarote and Tenerife: Naviera Armas and Trasmediterranea (between Arrecife, Lanzarote and Santa Cruz, Tenerife).

Between Fuerteventura and Gran Canaria: Navieras Armas (between Puerto del Rosario, Fuerteventura and Las Palmas de Gran Canaria); Navieras Armas and Trasmediterranea (between Morro Jable, Fuerteventura and Las Palmas de Gran Canaria); the Trasmditteranea sailing is on the fast JetFoil (1½ hours).

Between Fuerteventura and Tenerife: Trasmediterranea (between Morro Jable, Fuerteventura and Santa Cruz, Tenerife, via Las Palmas de Gran Canaria); Navieras Armas (between Puerto del Rosario, Fuerteventura and Santa Cruz, Tenerife via Las Palmas de Gran Canaria, Gran Canaria).

Between Gran Canaria and Tenerife: Líneas Fred Olsen (from Agaete, Gran Canaria and Santa Cruz, Tenerife); Naviera Armas and Trasmediterranea (from Las Palmas, Gran Canaria and Santa Cruz, Tenerife).

Between Gran Canaria and La Palma: Trasmediterranea (between Las Palmas, Gran Canaria and Santa Cruz de La Palma, La Palma.

Between Tenerife and El Hierro: Líneas. Fred Olsen and Trasmedi-terrannea (between Los Cristianos, Tenerife and Valverde, El Hierro).

Between Tenerife and La Gomera: Líneas Fred Olsen, Naviera Armas, Trasarmas, and Trasmediterranea (between Los Cristianos, Tenerife and San Sebastián de La Gomera.

Between Tenerife and La Palma: Líneas Fred Olsen and Trasmediterranea (between Los Cristianos, Tenerife and Santa Cruz de La Palma); Trasmediterranea (between Santa Cruz, Tenerif, and Santa Cruz de La Palma).

Between La Palma and La Gomera/El Hierro: Trasmediterranea (between Santa Cruz de La Palma, La Palma and Valverde, El Hierro via San Sebastián de La Gomera).

TAXIS

The letters SP (*servicio público*) on the front and rear bumpers of a car indicate that it is a taxi. It might also have a green light in the front windshield or a green sign indicating "libre" when it is available. Taxis are unmetered in tourist areas. There are fixed prices displayed on a board at the main taxi rank, giving the fares to the most popular destinations. These are reasonable. If in doubt, ask the driver before you set off.

TAXES

Impuestos Generalisado Indirecto Canario (IGIC) is levied on all bills at a rate of 4.5% as of January 2000.

TELEPHONES *(teléfono)*

In addition to the telephone office, Telefonica, <www.telefonica. es>, major towns and cities have phone booths everywhere for local and international calls. Instructions in English and area codes for different countries are displayed in the booths. International calls are expensive, so be sure to have a plentiful supply of 100 peseta coins. Some phones accept credit cards, and many require a phonecard *(tarjeta telefónica)*, available from tobacconists. For international direct dialing, wait for the dial tone, then dial 07, wait for a second tone and dial the country code, area code (minus the initial zero) and number.

Calling directly from your hotel room is almost always prohibitively expensive unless you are using a calling card, or some other similar system, from your local long distance supplier e.g. AT&T or MCI. Find out from the supplier the free connection number applicable to the countries (they are different for each country) you are travelling to before you leave, as these numbers are not always easily available once there.

A more recent and economic option, but one that is only readily available in the large cities and resorts, are private companies that have a number of booths in stores. These are usually highly competitive rates, and you pay at the completion of the call.

The number for the International Operator is 025.

The country code for the USA and Canada is 1; Great Britain 44; Australia 61; New Zealand 64; the Republic of Ireland 353, and South Africa 27.

Telephone Codes for the Canaries:

Province of Santa Cruz de Tenerife: Tenerife, El Hierro, La Gomera and La Palma: (telephone code 922).

Province of Las Palmas de Gran Canaria: Gran Canaria, Lanzarote and Fuerteventura: (telephone code 928).

TIME DIFFERENCES

In winter the Canaries maintain Greenwich Mean Time, which is one hour behind most European countries, including Spain. For the rest of the year the islands go on summer time, as does Spain — keeping the one-hour difference.

Winter time chart

Los Angeles	New York	London	**Canaries**	Madrid
4 a.m.	7 a.m.	noon	**noon**	1 p.m

TIPPING

Since a service charge is normally included in hotel and restaurant bills, tipping is not obligatory. Ten percent of the bill is usual for taxi drivers, bartenders, and waiters. Also tip others offering personal services.

TOILETS

The most commonly used expressions for toilets in the Canaries are *servicios* or *aseos*, though you may also hear or see WC, water, and *retretes*.

Public conveniences are rare, but most hotels, bars, and restaurants have toilets. It is considered polite to buy a coffee if you do drop into a bar just to use the toilet.

Where are the toilets?   **¿Dónde están los servicios?**

TOURIST INFORMATION OFFICES *(oficina de turismo)*

Information on the Canary Islands may be obtained from one of the international branches of the Spanish National Tourist Offices, as listed below.

Australia: Level 2–203 Castlereagh Street, NSW, 2000 Sydney South; Tel. (2) 2647966.

Canada: 2 Bloor Street West, 34th Floor, Toronto, Ontario M4W 3E2; Tel. (416) 961-3131; fax (416) 961-1992; e-mail spainto@ globalserve.net.

U.K.: 22-23 Manchester Square, London, W1M 5AP; Tel. (0171) 486-8077; fax (0171) 486-8034; e-mail buzon.oficial@londres. oet.mcx.es.

U.S.: Water Tower Place, Suite 915 East, 845 N. Michigan Avenue, Chicago, IL 60611; Tel. (312) 642-1992; fax (312) 642-9817; e-mail buzon.oficial@chicago.oet.mcx.es.

8383 Wilshire Boulevard, Suite 960, Beverly Hills, Los Angeles, CA 90211; Tel. (213) 658 7188; fax (323) 658-1061; e-mail buzon.oficial@losangeles.oet.mcx.es.

665 Fifth Avenue, New York, NY 10103; Tel. (212) 265-8822; fax (212) 265-8864, e-mail buzon.oficial@nuevayork.oet.mcx.es.

1221 Brickell Avenue, Miami, FL 33131; Tel. (305) 358-1992; fax (305) 358-8223; e-mail buzon.oficial@miami.oet.mcx.es.

Canary Islands

For further information check the Internet web site <www.tourspain.es>.

During your vacation, information on the islands may be obtained from any of the following local offices.

Province of Santa Cruz de Tenerife (telephone code 922):
Tenerife:

Santa Cruz de Tenerife: Cabildo Insular (Plaza de Espana); Tel. 23 95 92/23 98 11/23 92 63; fax 23 98 12; <www.cabtfe.es/.info/texto/e/indexnovaja.html>; open Monday–Friday 8am–6pm and Saturday 9am–1pm.

Adeje: Avda. Rafael Puig, 1 (across from the Playa de Troya); Tel/fax 75 06 33; open Monday–Frid 9am–2:30pm.

Aeropuerto Tenerife Sur Reina Sofia (Arrivals Terminal): Tel. 39 20 37; open Monday–Friday 9am–9pm and Saturday 9am–1pm.

Playa de Las Americas: Arona — across from the Hotel Palmeiras; Tel. 79 76 68; fax 75 71 98; open Monday 9am–3:30pm, Tuesday 9am–9pm, closed Wednesday–Thursday midday–3:30pm, Friday 9am–3:30pm and Saturday 9am–1pm.

Playa de Las Vistas: Tel.75 06 69; e-mail vistas@atlantis.es; open Monday–Friday 9am–5pm.

Candelaria/Las Caletillas: Avda. del Generalisimo, s/n; Tel. 50 04 15.

El Medano: Plaza de los Principes de Espana; Tel. 17 60 02; open Monday–Friday (summer) 9am–2pm, (winter) 9am–3pm and Saturday 9am–1pm.

La Laguna: Plaza del Adelantado; Tel. 63 11 94; open Monday–Saturday 8am–8pm.

La Oratova: Calle Carrera del Escultor Estevez, 2; Tel. 32 30 41; fax 32 11 42; open Monday–Friday 9am–6pm and Saturday 10am–2pm.

Las Galletas: Avda. Maritima; Tel. 73 01 33; open Monday–Friday 9am–3:30pm and Saturday 9am–1pm.

Los Cristianos: Centro Cultural (Casa de La Cultura), Calle General Franco, s/n (across from the Mobil gas station); Tel. 75 71 37; fax 75 24 92; open Monday–Friday 9am–3:30pm and Saturday 9am–1pm.

Puerto de La Cruz: Plaza de Europa, s/n; Tel. 38 60 00; fax 38 47 69; open Monday–Friday 9am–8pm (9am–7pm in Jul–Sept) and Saturday 9am–1pm.

Santiago del Teide: Centro Commercial "Seguro el Sol"(across from the Playa de la Arena), Calle Manuel Ravelo, 20–Local 35; Tel/fax 86 03 48; open Monday– Friday 9:30am–3:30pm and Saturday 9:30am–12:30pm.

El Hierro:
Valverde: Patronato Insular de Turismo, Calle Licenciado Bueno, 38900; Tel.55 03 02; fax 55 10 52; open Monday–Friday 8:30am–2:30pm and Saturday 9am–1pm.

La Gomera:
San Sebastián: Calle Real, 4; Tel. 14 01 47; fax 14 01 51; <www.La Gomera-island.com>; open Monday– Saturday 9am–1:30pm and 3:30pm–6pm and Sunday 10am– 1pm.

Playa de Santiago: Edificio Las Vistas, Local 8, Avda. Maritima, s/n; Tel. 89 56 50; fax 89 56 51; open Monday–Friday 9am–1pm and 4pm–7pm and Saturday 9am–1pm.

Valle Gran Rey: Calle Lepanto, s/n, La Playa; Tel/fax 80 54 58.

La Palma:
Santa Cruz de La Palma: Avda. Maritima, 3, 38700; Tel. 41 19 57; fax 42 00 30; open Monday–Friday 9am–1pm and 5pm–7pm and Saturday 10:30am–1pm.

Province of Las Palmas de Gran Canaria (telephone code 928).
Gran Canaria:
Las Palmas: Patronato de Turismo, León y Castilla, 17; Tel. 21 96 00; fax 21 96 01; <www.idecnet.com/patronatogc>; open Monday–

Canary Islands

Friday 8am–3pm and Parque de Santa Catalina, Plazoleta Ramón Franco, s/n; Tel. 26 46 23; open Monday–Friday 9am–3pm and Saturday 9am–1pm.

Maspalomas: Avda. de España corner of Avda. EE.UU; Tel. 76 25 91; fax 72 34 44; <www.maspalomas-web.org>; open Monday–Friday 9am–9pm and Saturday 9am–1pm.

Mogán: Centro Commercial (1st Phase); Tel. 56 00 29; fax 56 10 50; open Monday–Friday 9am–2:30pm.

Lanzarote:
Arrecife: Blas Cabrera Felipe, s/n; Tel. 80 24 75/80 21 59; fax 80 00 80.

Puerto del Carmen: On the promenade opposite Restaurante Playa Mar; Tel. 51 33 51; fax 83 39 56; <www.puertodelcarmen.com>; open Monday–Friday 10am–2pm and 6pm–8:30pm.

Costa Teguise: Between the Salinas Hotel and Lanzarote Beach Club; Tel. 59 08 10.

Playa Blanca: Muelle de Playa Blanca (in the port); Tel. 51 77 94; open Monday–Friday 9am–5pm.

Fuerteventura:
Puerto del Rosario: Calle 1º de Mayo, 33; Tel. 85 10 24; fax 85 18 12. Aeropuerto; Tel. 85 12 50.

Corralejo: Plaza Grande de Corralejo; Tel. 86 62 35; fax 86 61 86.

Morro Jable: In the shopping Center; Tel.54 07 76; fax 54 10 23.

TRAVELERS WITH DISABILITIES

There are wheelchair ramps at the major airports, and many larger apartments and hotels do make provision for disabled guests. Some of the more modern resorts also provide ramps to cross pavements. The facilities at Los Cristianos are renowned among disabled travelers and the Marisol Resort in particular specializes

for disabled travelers and their families. The streets of
s such as Santa Cruz de Tenerife and Las Palmas are
ult to negotiate, due to narrow, high pavements and lack
of parking space.

For general information on facilities for disabled travelers in the
Canary Islands, contact Federation ECOM; Balmes, 311 Ent. 2;
08006, Barcelona; (Tel. (93) 217 3882.

WATER *(agua)*

Tap water is safe to drink but is not recommended for its taste. The
Spaniards almost invariably drink bottled water.

WEB SITES

See TOURIST INFORMATION.

WEIGHTS AND MEASURES

The metric system is used in the Islands.

Length

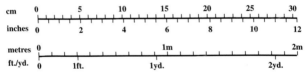

Weight

grams	0	100	200	300	400	500	600	700	800	900	1kg
ounces	0	4	8	12	1lb	20	24	28	2lb		

Temperature

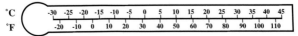

Recommended Hotels

Below is a selection of hotels in different price bands for each island. Book well in advance, particularly for *paradores* and if visiting the islands during the high season or during *Carnaval*. The star rating in brackets after each hotel name refers to the official government grading system (see page 103). As a basic guide to room prices we have used the following symbols (for a double room with bath/shower in high season):

$$$$$$	Over 100,000 ptas, €601.01
$$$$$	50,000–100,000 ptas, €300.51–601.01
$$$$	30,000–50,000 ptas, €180.30–300.51
$$$	20,000–30,000 ptas, €120.20–180.30
$$	10,000–20,000 ptas, €60.10–120.20
$	below 10,000 ptas, €60.10

PROVINCE OF SANTA CRUZ DE TENERIFE

Tenerife

Hotel Botánico (5 stars GL) $$$$ *Avda. Richard J. Yeoward, 1, 38400 Puerto de La Cruz; Tel. 38 14 00; fax 38 15 04; <www.hotelbotanico.com>*. In 2½ hectares (6 acres) of gardens and parklands, it has an elegant and peaceful atmosphere with views over the Atlantic Ocean and Mount Teide. Four restaurants, bars, boutiques and a health center. 251 rooms.

Atalaya Gran Hotel (4 stars) $$$ *Parque Taoro, Apdo. 250, 38400 Puerto de La Cruz; Tel. 38 44 51; fax 38 70 46*. Traditional family style hotel with stunning views over the town and coast, and in its own huge tropical garden. Some rooms are handicapped accessible. Large heated pool, sporting opportunities and free entry to the Casino. 183 rooms.

Hotel-Residencia Regulo (1 star) $ *Calle Pérez Zamora, 16, 38400 Puerto de La Cruz; Tel. 38 45 06; fax 37 04 20.* A small, but rather stylish little hotel right in the center of Puerto, near the port itself. No parking. 14 rooms.

Hotel San Roque (3 stars) $$$ *Calle Esteban de Ponte, 32, 38450 Garachico; Tel. 13 34 35; fax 13 34 06; <www.hotelsan-roque.com>.* A beguiling and eclectic mix of a traditional 17th-century palace with traditional wooden beamed ceilings and balconies and modernizations such as CD's, satellite TV and even Jacuzzi tubs. Pool set in a charming patio. 20 rooms.

Parador de Cañadas del Teide (3 stars) $$$ *38300 La Orotava; Tel. 38 64 15; fax 38 23 52; e-mail canadas@ parador.es.* Located in the rugged area directly under El Teide and next to the unusual peaks of Los Roques. Close to the cable car. Decorated in Canary Islands style, best to opt for half board. 23 rooms.

Gran Hotel Bahia del Duque, Gran Meliá (5 stars Gran Luxo GL) $$$$ *Calle Alcade Walter Paetzmann, s/n, 38660 Costa Adeje; Tel. 74 69 00; fax 74 69 25; <www.bahia-duque.com>.* An amazingly eclectic array of buildings, all of which surround a subtropical assemblage of fantastic gardens, pools, restaurants and bars that drop over several levels to the beach. Traditionally dressed staff, peacocks roam free and an amazing lobby that will impress almost anyone. 362 rooms.

Flamingo Suites $$$$/$$$$$ *Avda. España, s/n, Playa de las Américas; Tel. 71 84 00; fax 71 84 01; <www.flamingo-tener-ife.com>.* Luxury apartments in the heart of Playa de las Américas; in fact this is considered Tenerife's most exclusive private club. Every modern facility, including Jacuzzi tubs, pools and daily maid service. 18 suites.

Canary Islands

Grand Hotel Anthelia Park (4 stars) $$$ *Calle Londres, s/n, Playas del Duque, 38670 Costa Adeje; Tel. 71 33 35; fax 71 90 81; <www.anthelia-park.com>.* A huge and modern complex in both style and ambiance. Every comfort in the rooms, restaurants, bars, shops, pools, and wonderful views over the beach; the entrance to Puerto Colón and La Gomera in the distance.

Arona Gran Hotel (4 stars) $$ *Los Cristianos; Tel. 75 06 78; fax 75 02 43.* On the beach at the end of Los Cristianos harbor, all rooms are modern and with a terrace overlooking the water. Sports facilities, restaurants and bars, and a wonderful atrium lobby totally bedecked with green plants hanging from each floor. Excellent value. 400 rooms.

Hotel Rural Finca Salamanca $$ *Ctra. Güimar-El Puertito, Km. 1.5; Tel. 51 45 30; fax 51 40 61; <www.hotel-fincasalamanca.com>.* A rarity in Tenerife, an antique manor house, in a country estate, that has been converted into a charming small hotel for those who want to enjoy peace and quiet and still enjoy top class facilities. 16 rooms.

El Hierro

Parador El Hierro (3 stars) $$$ *Las Playas, El Hierro; Tel. 55 80 36; fax 55 80 86; e-mail hiero@parador.es.* Found in an isolated location by the beach and under the mountains, this charming parador has recently been totally renovated. 47 rooms.

La Gomera

Jardín Tecina Hotel (4 stars) $$$ *Lomada de Tecina, 38810 Playa de Santiago; Tel. 14 58 50; fax 14 58 51.* A stylish complex set in its own extensive gardens on the cliffs. An ambiance of easygoing friendliness combined with the peace and beauty of the surroundings makes it a fantastic hideaway. Also an array of restaurants, bars, pools, numerous sports facilities and the hotel's own beach club. 434 rooms.

Conde de la Gomera Parador (4 stars) $$$ *38800 San Sebastián de La Gomera; Tel. 8 11 00; fax 87 11 16; <www.parador.es/cgi-bin/tes?en&gomera>.* A comfortable country manor beautifully furnished in a style that combines Castilian and Isabelline influences. It has a superb cliff-top site overlooking San Sebastián and with views across to Tenerife and Mount Teide. 58 rooms.

Hotel Gran Rey (3 stars) $$ *La Puntilla, s/n, 38870, Valle Gran Rey; Tel. 80 58 59, fax 80 56 51; <www.hotel-granrey.com>.* Across from the beach and facing the fishing port this is the only hotel of note in this part of La Gomera. Elongated and modern in design, it has a rooftop pool with delightful rooms. 99 rooms.

La Palma

Parador de la Palma (4 stars) $$ *El Zumacal, 38720 Breña Baja; Tel. 43 58 28; fax 43 59 99; e-mail lapalma@parador.es.* A new parador located on the cliffs just to the south of, and over-looking, Santa Cruz. Traditional Canarian in style and décor with a delightful central patio, this has spacious rooms and pleasant gardens with a pool. 78 rooms.

Hotel Sol Elite La Palma (4 stars) $$$ *Playa de Puerto de Naos, 38760 Los Llanos de Aridane; Tel. 40 80 00; fax 40 80 14; e-mail sol.elite.la.palma@solmelia.es.* A modern beach-side hotel, and one of the few hotels of size on the west coast of the island. Every facility including restaurants, bars, swimming pools, and sports. 307 rooms.

Hotel La Palma Romántica (3 stars) $$ *Crta. General Las Llanadas, 38726 Barlovento; Tel. 18 62 61; fax 18 64 00; <www.wintercom.es/sisentis/palmarom>.* In the northeast of the island, a modern building with a traditional architectural style and beautiful views. Very pleasant rooms, restaurant, bodega, sauna, outdoor and indoor pool, whirlpool, and Turkish bath. 34 rooms.

PROVINCE OF LAS PALMAS DE GRAN CANARIA

Gran Canaria

Hotel Reina Isabel (5 stars) $$$ Calle *Alfredo L. Jones, 40, 35008 Las Palmas; Tel. 26 01 00; fax 27 45 58*. The capital's highly rated and centrally located hotel on the famous Playas de Las Canteras beach. Excellent 8th floor restaurant with panoramic views, roof-top pool, and nightclub. 233 rooms.

Sol Bardinos (4 stars) $$ *Eduardo Benot, 5, 35007 Las Palmas; Tel. 27 00 00, fax 22 91 39*. Found in the easily identifiable round tower, the only skyscraper in this part of town, and close to the Playa de Las Canteras. Modern rooms with a pool on the top floors and restaurant on the 24th floor. 215 rooms.

Steigenberger La Canaria (5 stars) $$$$$ *35120 Arguineguin; Tel. 15 04 00; fax 15 10 03; <www.steigenberger.com>*. One of the newest and most luxurious hotels on the south coast. Cut into a cliff with its own private gardens, access to beaches, gourmet restaurant and health center. This has excellent facilities and breathtaking sea views. 244 rooms.

Hotel Taurito Princess (4 stars) $$$ *Urb. Playa de Taurito, 35138 Mogán; Tel. 56 51 80; fax 56 55 66*. This sits on a cliff surrounded by a pretty bay and the delightful pool complex of *Largo Taurito*. All modern rooms have sea views, an array of restaurants, bars, sports facilities, pools, sauna and massage. 404 rooms.

Hotel Club de Mar (3 stars) $$ *Urbanización Puerto de Mogán, s/n, 35140, Playa de Mogán; Tel. 56 50 66; fax 56 54 38; <www.clubdemar.com>*. An absolutely wonderful location at the end of the harbor in this delightful marina. Pleasant rooms with all expected facilities, pool and bar and swimming in the harbor. 56 twin rooms.

Apartamentos Club de Mar (2 stars) \$\$ *Puerto de Mogán, s/n, 35140, Playa de Mogán; Tel. 56 50 66; fax 56 54 38.* In the beautiful marina of Puerto Mogán, designed to blend in with the local town-house style. These have a twin bedroom, sofa bed in lounge, balcony and rooftop terrace, with use of hotel facilities. 95 apartments.

Hotel Princesa Guayarmina \$ *Los Berrazales, s/n (El Valle), 35480 Agaete; Tel. 89 80 09; fax 89 85 25.* Situated at the end of a lush valley at 325 m (1,066 ft) above sea level and dedicated to health and relaxation. The *Los Berraxales* health center provides numerous natural treatments, and the restaurant specializes in both Canarian and vegetarian dishes. 33 rooms.

Lanzarote

Hotel Gran Meliá Salinas (five stars) \$\$\$\$\$ *Avda. Islas Canarias, s/n, 35509, Costa Teguise; Tel. 59 00 40; fax 59 03 90; <www.solmelia.es>.* The island's largest and most luxurious hotel, and part of the *Cultural Heritage of Lanzarote.* A stunning double atrium filled with magnificent indoor gardens and waterfalls — artistic interpretations, as is the pool, of César Manrique. Over 300 rooms.

The Garden Villas, Gran Meliá Salinas \$\$\$\$\$\$ *Avda. Islas Canarias, s/n, 35509, Costa Teguise; Tel. 59 00 40; fax 59 03 90; <www.solmelia.es>.* These ten villas, a hotel within a hotel, are in their own private grounds around a large pool. Each one epitomizes absolute luxury and privacy, with four-poster canopy beds (you can even select the types of sheets and pillows you prefer), its own private pool, 24-hour butler service and every other type of luxury you could ever wish for.

Hotel Los Fariones (4 stars) \$\$\$ *Roque del Este, 1 35510 Puerto del Carmen; Tel. 51 01 75; fax 51 02 02; e-mail fariones@infolanz.es.* A long-established family hotel on a fine beach with its own secluded cove and large pool. Quiet atmosphere, central location, and excellent service. Sports center just 91 m (100 yards) away. 242 rooms.

Hotel Timanfaya Palace (4 stars) $$ *Playa Blanca, 35570 Yaiza; Tel. 51 76 76; fax 51 70 35; <www.h10.es>.* A stunning example of Hispanic/Arabic modern architecture; immense lobby with fountains, pools and waterfalls under a huge wooden-beamed ceiling; views to Fuerteventura. Every modern amenity as well as restaurants, bars, ballroom, two pools, open-air Jacuzzi, and nudist area. 315 rooms.

Fuerteventura

Hotel Riu Palace Tres Islas (4 stars) $$$ *Grandes Playas, 35660 Corralejo; Tel. 53 57 00; fax 53 58 58.* Perfectly located on a magnificent beach with a view of the dunes and Lanzarote. Well appointed rooms, attractive pool and terrace, boutiques, and nightly entertainment in the piano bar and *Betancuria* lounge. 365 rooms.

Sol Elite Gorriones (4 stars) $$$ *Playa Barca, 35628 Pájara; Tel. 54 70 25; fax 54 70 00; e-mail sol-elite.gorriones@solmelia.es.* Recently renovated, this sits in an absolutely isolated location alongside one of the best beaches on the island; an ideal beach getaway. Most rooms have a terrace with sea views. 431 rooms.

Hotel Fuerteventura (3 stars) $$ *Playa Blanca, 45, 35600 Puerto del Rosario; Tel. 85 11 50; fax 85 11 58.* Opened in 1999 on a deserted beach just south of Puerto del Rosario. Easily identifiable by its unusual green central tower, this has all the service and facilities that the *paradores* are renowned for.

Barceló Club El Castillo $$ *Caleta de Fuste, 35610 El Castillo; Tel. 16 31 01; fax 16 30 42; elcastillo@barcelo.com.* A group of 382 units of one or two story bungalows all of which are fully equipped and have either a garden or sea view. Numerous bars, restaurants, and sports facilities, and other forms of entertainment.

Recommended Restaurants

We appreciated the food and service in the restaurants listed below; if you find other places that you think are worth recommending, we'd be pleased to hear from you.

To give you an idea of price (per person; a three-course meal including half a bottle of house wine), we have used the following symbols:

$$$$	Over 5,000 ptas, €30.05
$$$	3,000–5,000 ptas, €18.03–30.05
$$	1,500–3,000 ptas, €9.02–18.02
$	under 1,500 ptas, €9.02

PROVINCE OF SANTA CRUZ DE TENERIFE

Tenerife

The Oriental $$$$ *Avda. Richard J. Yeoward, 1, Puerto de la Cruz; Tel. 38 14 00; fax 38 15 04.* Within the Hotel Botánico, the specialty is Thai cookery with Pan-Asiatic touches. The ambiance here is formal, jacket and tie for gentlemen are obligatory, and the cuisine is enticing. Open for dinner every evening of the year.

Casa de Miranda $$ *Calle Santo Domingo, 13 (Plaza de Europa), Puerto de La Cruz; Tel. 37 38 71.* This charming old Canarian house with wooden beams, floors and staircases dates from 1730. The *bodeguita* on the lower floor, with the restaurant, specialties meats, fish and shellfish, upstairs. Bogeguita open 8am–midnight and restaurant 1pm–11:30pm.

Régulo $$ *Calle Pérez Zamora, 16, Puerto de la Cruz; Tel. 38 45 06; fax 37 04 20.* Located within a typical Canarian 18th-century house with balconies around a charming patio. Specialties include *Lapas a la plancha* (grilled limpet shells) and *Solomillo* *relleno de camembert* (filet steak with camembert stuffing). Open for lunch and dinner, closed Sundays and for the month of July.

Mi Vaca y Yo $$$ *Calle Cruz Verde, 3, Puerto de la Cruz; Tel. 38 52 47.* Superb international cuisine in an exotic sub-tropical setting. A great favorite with tourists. Open for lunch and dinner but closed in June.

Restaurante Los Arcos $$$ *Ctra. General, 254, Tacoronte; Tel. 56 09 65.* Just north of Tacoronte, this restaurant celebrated its 25th anniversary in 1997 with a menu at 1972 prices. Expect an interesting mix of fish and meat dishes, along with the house speciality — fondue. The dishes are for two people, and include meat, vegetable, fish, cheese, and wine fondues.

Parador de Cañadas del Teide $$$ *38300, La Orotava; Tel. 38 64 15; fax 38 23 52; e-mail canadas@parador.es.* A traditional style dining room with spectacular views of Mount Teide. Canarian dishes such as *Puchero Canaria* (Canary Style Stew) and *Conejo al Salmorejo* (Marinated rabbit).

Hotel San Roque $$$ *Calle Esteban de Ponte, 32, Garachico; Tel. 13 34 35; <www.hotelsanroque.com>.* Eat in a small dining room or at tables around the pool. The cuisine is as eclectic as the ambiance. Expect to find such delicacies as *daurade au sel* (fish baked on rock salt) and *paella duo* (made with vegetables and squid).

Restaurante-bar Mirador "La Fuente" $$ *Bajada a la Plaza, Masca; Tel. 86 34 66.* In the village just below the road, and with marvelous views through the mountains, this has a variety of local produce on sale, as well as basic Canarian dishes.

Restaurante a la Carta Poseidón $$$ *Calle Londres, s/n, Playas del Duque, 38670 Costa Adeje; Tel. 71 33 35.* The haute-cuisine restaurant of the Grand Hotel Anthelia Park. Beautifully presented, interesting dishes such as smoked salmon with hand made goat's cheese, tender fillets of sole stuffed with extremely tasty small shrimps and spinach, and Charlottes.

Restaurante La Tasca, Gran Hotel Bahia del Duque, Gran Meliá $$$ *Calle Alcade Walter Paetzmann, s/n, 38660 Costa Adeje; Tel. 74 69 00; fax 74 69 25.* A Spanish restaurant in décor, style and cuisine, with staff in traditional costumes. Familiar dishes, and some less so, are on the menu.

El Sol $$$ *Transversal General Franco, s/n, Los Cristianos; Tel. 79 05 69.* Classic French cuisine is the specialty of the house in this highly recommended restaurant. Open for dinner only, closed Monday–May and during June.

El Hierro

Mirador de la Peña $$ *Ctra. Gral.Guarazoca, 40, Valverde;. Tel. 55 03 00.* Another *mirador* restaurant to benefit from the Manrique treatment. Island specialties are served in a tranquil, modern room with wonderful views.

La Gomera

Restaurante El Laurel $$$$ *Lomada de Tecina, 38810 Playa de Santiago; Tel. 14 58 50; fax 14 58 51.* The a-la-carte restaurant of the Jardín Tecina resort. By the beach, and reached by elevator through the cliffs. A fantastic location combined with a romantic ambiance, guitarists and, of course, *haute cuisine* and fine wines. Easily the best restaurant on the island.

Las Rosas Restaurant $$ *Carretera General, Las Rosas; Tel. 80 09 16.* Panoramic views of Tenerife and Mount Teide and good, typical Gomeran cuisine. When coach parties arrive, demonstrations of *el Silbo*, the island's whistling language, are given. Open daily, midday–3:30pm.

Conde de la Gomera Parador $$$ *38800 San Sebastián de La Gomera; Tel. 87 11 00; fax 87 11 16.* Excellent Canarian food such as *cazuela de pescados gomeros* (fish casserole), *lomos de conejo rellenos* (stuffed rabbit loin) and *potaje de berros* (watercress broth), served in colonial-style surroundings.

Restaurante Escuela Mirador César Manrique $$$ *Carretera General de Arure, 38870 Valle Gran Rey; Tel. 80 58 68.* A very dramatic position overlooking the steep mountainsides of the head of the Valle Gran Rey. Worth a stop just for the view. Open Wednesday–Sunday from 10am–10:30pm, with the dining room open 12:30pm–4pm and 6:30pm–10pm.

Bar-Pizzeria Avenida $$ *Playa Santiago; Tel. 89 54 98.* A very pleasant small restaurant in this totally unspoiled little town. A fine selection of fresh fish, that can be eaten inside or on tables across the road, over looking the beach.

La Palma

Parador de la Palma $$$ *El Zumacal, 38720 Breña Baja; Tel. 43 58 28; fax 43 59 99; e-mail lapalma@parador.es.* Sample traditional dishes like *caldo de trigo con coles abiertas* (corn soup with cabbage), *las chayotas rellenas de carne de cabra* (chayotes stuffed with goat's meat), and *el conejo en mojo hervido* (boiled rabbit in a typical sauce).

Restaurante La Placeta $$$ *Borrero, 1; Tel. 41 52 73; fax 41 66 92.* Located in a charming old house, this has a delightful ambiance. Wooden floors, beams, staircase, and old windows complement home-cooked International style cuisine with an emphasis on fish, meats and sauces. Open daily from 7pm–11pm.

Restaurante/bar La Gaviota $ *Piscinas de la Fajana, Barlovento; Tel. 18 60 99.* A neat restaurant with a great location overlooking the salt-water swimming pools built into the rocks. Views to the north where the cliffs fall into the ocean are spectacular. The menú del dia is only 1,400 ptas, €8.41 and it is open daily from 9am–midnight.

Restaurante El Faro $ *Tel. 44 40 51. El Faro.* Located in an isolated fishermen's cove. No more than a shack with a tin roof, plastic seats and tables, and sand floor. What it lacks in style it more than makes up for in the freshest fried fish, and a delightful ambiance with endless views over the Atlantic Ocean.

GRAN CANARIA

Restaurante Gurufer $$$ *Calle León y Castilla, 274, 35005 Las Palmas; Tel. 24 40 07; fax 23 47 09; e-mail gurufer@idecnet.com.* In one of the most distinguished old houses in town, this has a very classical ambiance and cuisine to match. A very tasteful menu that specializes in old-fashioned Canarian dishes, and fine wines.

Restaurante Cocina Vasco-Francesca $$$ *Tomás Miller, 73, Las Palmas; Tel. 27 57 52.* Follow the local custom, sit at the bar and select from tempting *tapas*. Try the delicious *Morcillo de Burgos* (black sausage from Burgos) or the more usual *gambas ajillos* (shrimp in boiling garlic) with the latter, of course, mopped up with bread.

Restaurante-Meson La Silla $$ *Ctra. La Silla, 9, Artenara; Tel. 66 61 08.* Enter through a tunnel cut through the rock and be met by the most stupendous views of a very dramatic valley. Reasonable food at reasonable prices and one of the best views on the island.

Restaurante El Senador $$$ *Paseo del Faro, s/n, Playa de Maspalomas; Tel. 14 04 96.* Overlooking the wide beach at Maspalomas, casual at lunch but formal for dinner. Specialties include *Arroz con bogovante o la marinera* (Rice pot with lobster or seafood) and *Caldereta de langosta al estilo de Menorca* (Spiny lobster casserole Menorcan style). Open every day.

Restaurante Hotel Club de Mar $$ *Urbanización Puerto de Mogán, s/n, 35140, Playa de Mogán; Tel. 56 50 66; fax 56 54 38; <www.clubdemar.com>.* In a town of many restaurants, this has one of the best locations. Wide ranging menu with, of course, "Mogán" fresh fish.

Lanzarote

Restaurante "La Graciosa" $$$$ *Avda. Islas Canarias, s/n, 35509, Costa Teguise; Tel. 59 00 40; fax 59 03 90; <www.solmelia .es>.* The a-la-carte restaurant of the Gran Meliá Salinas is as sumptious as you would expect. Dishes include goose breast with French beans, breast of chicken with a parfait of liver, sauce of truf-fles and raisins, and some interesting vegetarian dishes.

Freiduria-Bar La Lonja $$ *Calle Varadero, s/n, Puerto del Carmen; Tel. 51 13 77.* An attractive modern two-level building with a high, decorated ceiling and marine theme. A wonderful tapas bar and fresh fish shop on the ground floor, and a restaurant offering the very best grilled fish and shellfish on the second. Open every day.

Restaurante Casa Roja $$ *Calle Varadero, s/n, Puerto del Carmen; Tel. 17 32 63.* A charming ochre-red building that sits, literally, right over the harbor waters. Look for a small bar, delightful inside dining rooms, and a wonderful terrace just above the water overlooking the boats moored in the harbor. Fish and shellfish are the house specialty.

Jardín de Cactus $$ *Guatiza; Tel. 52 93 97.* Good, simple Canarian lunches are served on a peaceful terrace shaded by an awning overlooking the nice gardens, lunch only. Open every day.

La Era $$$ *Yaiza; Tel. 83 00 16.* A charming 300-year old typical Canarian country house, with a whitewashed courtyard decked with flowers, that serves outstanding island specialties. There is also an art-filled, wooden-beamed bar that serves snacks and light meals, and a craft shop. Yet another César Manrique creation.

Montañas del Fuego Restaurante "El Diablo" $$ *Montañas del Fuego, Parque Nacional de Timanfaya; Tel. 84 00 57.* Order grilled food and watch it cooked on a barbecue heated naturally by the volcano, then eat it in a pleasant round restaurant that has large picture windows with views over the lava fields. Open every day from midday–3:30pm.

Bar Restaurante "La Casita" $$ *Calle La Balita, 8, Playa Quemada; Tel. 17 32 63*; Just off the beach in this small community, it has a décor of nets, other fishing equipment and antiques, and a tiny two-person bar. Typical Canarian dishes and fish barbecues are served on a terrace with marvelous views of the ocean and cliffs.

Fuerteventura

Hotel Fuerteventura $$$ *Playa Blanca, 45, Puerto del Rosario; Tel. 85 1 50; fax 85 11 58.* Found just south of Puerto del Rosario, overlooking a secluded beach, this offers the traditionally high level of the parador chain and specializes in regional fish and goat.

Restaurante Escuela El Molina de Antigua $$ *Centro de Artesanía Molino de Antigua, Antigua; Tel. 87 82 20.* Typical local cuisine is served in the atmospheric outbuildings next to the windmill that gives this restaurant its name.

Restaurante Valtarajal $$ *Calle Roberto Roldán, s/n, Betancuria; Tel. 87 80 07.* A small, pleasantly decorated restaurant that specializes in Canarian stew, goat meat, majorero (small goat), Canarian potatoes, and Majorero cheese. Open every day, 9am–9pm.

INDEX